THE EVERYTHING®
ROTTWEILER
BOOK

D0011886

A complete guide to raising, training, and
caring for your Rottweiler

Margaret Holowinski

Adams Media
Avon, Massachusetts

Dedication:

In Memory of Snopeak Kiana of Sky Warrior CGC, NA, U-AGI, WPD, WTD, PDX, A-PDX. You're sorely missed.

Publishing Director: Gary M. Krebs
Managing Editor: Kate McBride
Copy Chief: Laura MacLaughlin
Acquisitions Editor: Bethany Brown
Development Editor: Lesley Bolton
Production Editor: Jamie Wielgus

Production Director: Susan Beale
Production Manager: Michelle Roy Kelly
Series Designers: Daria Perreault and John Paulhus
Cover Design: Paul Beatrice, Frank Rivera
Layout and Graphics: Colleen Cunningham
Rachael Eiben, Michelle Roy Kelly,
John Paulhus, Daria Perreault, Erin Ring

An Everything® Series Book.
Everything® and everything.com® are registered trademarks of F+W Publications, Inc.

Published by Adams Media, an F+W Publications Company
57 Littlefield Street, Avon, MA 02322 U.S.A.
www.adamsmedia.com

ISBN: 1-59337-122-5
Printed in Canada.

J   I   H   G   F   E   D   C   B   A

Library of Congress Cataloging-in-Publication Data
Holowinski, Margaret.
The everything rottweiler book / Margaret Holowinski.
p.   cm. — (An everything series book)
ISBN 1-59337-122-5
1.   Rottweiler dog. I. Title. II. Series: Everything series.

SF429.R7H66 2004
636.73—dc22

2004002377

Interior photographs by Kent and Donna Dannen,
1997 Big Owl Road, Allenspark, CO 80510

This book is available at quantity discounts for bulk purchases.
For information, call 1-800-872-5627.

Height:

Dogs: 24 to 27 inches; Bitches: 22 to 25 inches.

Weight:

Not listed in standard. Range approximately 70–120 pounds.

Head:

A rottweiler should have a strong, powerful head with broad jaws. His head (without the muzzle) should be about twice the length of the dog's entire muzzle. The forehead should not have wrinkles except when the dog looks alert.

Ears:

Rottweiler ears should look like they're alert and should be triangular. The ear should be no longer than mid-cheek.

Feet:

Feet should be compact so that they look round if you drew an outline around them. Feet should be straight when the dog stands. Toenails should be black. The back paws are slightly bigger than the front paws, still round, and should be straight when the dog stands.

Tail:

Tail docked short, close to the body, leaving one or two tail vertebrae.

Coat:

Coat should be coarse, dense, and medium length with an undercoat.

Topline:

The back is firm and level, extending in a straight line from behind the withers (shoulders) to the croup (base of tail). The back remains horizontal to the ground while the dog is moving or standing.

Movement:

Rottweilers are powerful trotters. Any other gait is not acceptable.

Temperament:

Rottweilers are calm and confident. He may be aloof, but will submit to inspection by a judge. Shyness or aggression in the ring isn't permitted and any dog that attacks a person in the ring is disqualified.

Acknowledgments

A huge thanks to my agent, Jessica Faust, of Bookends, Inc;
Diane Garnett from the American Rottweiler Club for permission
to reprint the rottweiler standard; Kent Dannen for the rottweiler
photos; and my husband, Larry, who encourages me
and acts as part-time editor.

• • •

Contents

Introduction

▶ SO, YOU WANT TO KNOW EVERYTHING about rottweilers? "Everything" is a tall order when it comes to these dogs. As a breed, rotties enjoyed relative anonymity until the 1980s, when their popularity and subsequent numbers skyrocketed. Yet even as the rottweiler became popular, rottweiler lovers of the breed warned people that these dogs weren't for everyone. Rottweilers need a gentle but firm hand in training, and owning a big, protective dog requires responsibility. Even so, rottweilers remained popular.

Their popularity is now on the decline, having dropped from within the top ten to number thirteen in the list of the most popular registered breeds. Part of this is due to the rottweiler's misrepresentation as a vicious breed, and part is due to breed bans (laws against owning a breed) enacted by municipalities. It is partly due to substandard dogs being churned out by puppy mills and backyard breeders. And the decline is also partly due to the conscientious responsible breeders who have educated the public that a rottweiler is not a dog for everyone.

Rotties are protective of their owners and property. They are often reserved or aloof with strangers, but many are cuddlers, too. Rottweilers must be socialized and trained properly. With a rottweiler comes great responsibility—a responsibility anyone with a big dog must accept.

This book will help guide you in selecting the perfect rottie for you and your family. You'll learn about the rottweiler and his unique history, as well as what makes the rottweiler different from other breeds. You'll learn how to find the best rottweiler in terms of health and temperament. You'll find out about the hereditary diseases that plague the rottweiler, many of which also plague other popular dogs. You'll also learn if a rescue rottie might be in your future.

Once you get your rottweiler home, you'll need to know how to survive the first few days and nights with your new pet.

Housebreaking doesn't mean breaking the house! You'll learn the quickest method in training your rottie to learn house manners.

Again, training and socialization is vitally important to your ability to keep and enjoy your rottweiler. Without proper training, your rottweiler could become uncontrollable. Without proper socialization, he won't have the means to tell what is normal in his environment and what is dangerous or frightening. Socialization and training are key commitments for every rottie owner.

You'll also learn how to care for your rottweiler and recognize symptoms to various diseases and ailments. What you feed your rottweiler has a lot of bearing on his health and well-being, and here you'll get the low-down on what food is good for your dog. This book also covers what to expect in the later years of your rottie's life and how long he can live.

While owning a rottie means work and responsibility, it is also a lot of fun. In addition to everyday play, you can also learn how to have fun by participating in various activities such as herding, conformation, obedience, Schutzhund, or agility. Even traveling with your rottie can be a pleasant experience; you'll soon learn how.

Does this book cover everything about rottweilers? Well, perhaps not *everything,* but it's pretty close, especially in areas that pertain to having a rottweiler as a pet. This book is not a guide for the show person—you won't find lists of famous stud dogs or any information about breeding your rottie.

You'll find resources throughout this book, plus helpful tips and facts. The information provided here will make your life easier and make your rottweiler relationship that much more enjoyable. If you're still not sure if the rottweiler is the right dog for you, this book is. (E)

Meet the Rottweiler

THE ROTTWEILER IS a versatile, loving, and caring pet. No doubt you've been drawn to the rottie because of his impressive good looks and his natural guarding ability. But the rottie isn't just a tough guy. Rottweilers have their tender side, too. This tender side can make the rottie an ideal pet for your home while still letting him be the rough-and-ready companion. But how much do you know about the rottie? Do you know where he came from and how his temperament is? In this chapter, we'll explore what makes the rottweiler.

Rugged and Ready—The Versatile Rottie

The rottweiler is a member of the American Kennel Club's (AKC's) Working Group, meaning he was originally bred to do a job. Rottweilers excel in work, whether it is herding, guarding, or obedience. Clever and capable of a variety of tasks, rotties are big dogs. Big dogs do big jobs.

Rottweilers are go-anywhere, do-anything dogs. They excel in obedience, agility, herding, and Schutzhund. They're protective and good at guarding their owners' families and possessions. They've worked as war dogs and police dogs. With such versatility, it's no wonder they've been very popular dogs, ranking in the top ten for years.

▲ With well-defined features, rottweilers are regal in appearance.

A Brief History of the Rottweiler

The rottweiler is from Germany. Although the breed's origins are shrouded in antiquity, most experts believe that the rottie was originally descended from Roman mastiffs, large and powerful dogs often used as guard dogs. It is believed that rottweilers were bred to protect and drive livestock to feed the great Roman legions, somewhere around A.D. 74. In later times, the rottweiler was still used as a drover dog, herding livestock from the barn to the fields in the morning and back to the barn at night.

Somewhere around A.D. 700, the town of Das Rote Wil ("the Red Tile") obtained its name from the red clay tiles unearthed from a Roman bathhouse. Eventually, its name became Rottweil, an obvious derivative. Rottweil became a trading point for livestock, and the drover dogs we know today as rottweilers became useful animals within the community. They drove cattle and pulled dog-carts. As these working dogs became popular, they were given the name rottweiler Metzerhund, or "Rottweil's butcher dogs."

In the nineteenth century, driving cattle in Germany was outlawed, and the rottweiler was in danger of disappearing. However, in 1901, the rottweiler began to gain favor as a police dog. The newly formed German rottweiler club registered 3,400 rottweilers, and the club published its first stud book in 1924.

 **fact**

Even with their popularity on the decline, the rottweiler is still a very popular breed, ranking thirteenth among registered breeds, with 22,196 registrations with the AKC in 2003. The first rottweiler registered with the AKC was Stina v Felsenmeer in 1931.

Through both World War I and II, the rottweiler continued to gain in popularity in Germany. But the breed remained relatively unknown in the United States until the early 1980s, when its popularity skyrocketed—at one point becoming the second most popular breed. Since then, the rottweiler has continued to enjoy popularity, now number thirteen in AKC registrations.

The AKC Rottweiler Standard

What is a standard? Standards are talked about in school, business, and sports, but when it comes to dogs, the concept might be a bit perplexing. You might think that the standard has to do with the quality of your puppy. After all, shouldn't your rottweiler be the very best you can buy?

When talking about dogs, a standard is a kind of blueprint for the breed. A dog is said to conform to the standard when he meets the requirements for that standard. Dogs that closely conform to the standard of their breed are considered show quality. The AKC adopted its first rottweiler standard in 1935.

No rottweiler actually conforms 100 percent to the standard. The standard is the idealized form of the dog—that is, what the experts have decided about how the rottweiler should look and behave. The American Rottweiler Club draws up and approves the rottweiler standard, which the AKC then approves. When you go over a standard, you'll read about toplines, withers, scissors bite, and various other terms. *The Complete Dog Book,* by the AKC, can give you definitions of these terms.

 **Question?**

How is show quality different from pet quality?
A show-quality dog is one that conforms more closely to the breed standard. A pet-quality dog is in no way inferior to a show-quality dog. However, the dog may have a physical fault or disqualification that prohibits him from being shown in the conformation show ring.

How important is the standard? Well, without a standard, a rottweiler might eventually end up looking nothing like a rottweiler at all! Given his background, he might start looking like a mastiff, or he might come out as just an average mutt. Because the rottweiler has been extremely popular, you'll find that many people breed rottweilers for profit, without any regard to the standard. This is why you may see rottweilers that don't look quite right or that have temperament problems. Reputable rottweiler breeders produce dogs that *look* and *act* like rottweilers. These breeders have an eye on producing quality puppies for pets, for show, and for work.

General Appearance

The ideal Rottweiler is a medium large, robust, and powerful dog, black with clearly defined rust markings. His compact and substantial build denotes great strength, agility, and endurance. Dogs are characteristically more massive throughout with larger frame and heavier bone than bitches. Bitches are distinctly feminine, but without weakness of substance or structure.

Size, Proportion, Substance

Dogs: 24 inches to 27 inches. Bitches: 22 inches to 25 inches, with preferred size being mid-range of each sex. Correct proportion is of primary importance, as long as size is within the standard's range.

The length of body, from prosternum to the rearmost projection of the rump, is slightly longer than the height of the dog at the withers, the most desirable proportion of the height to length being 9 to 10. The Rottweiler is neither coarse nor shelly. Depth of chest is approximately 50 percent of the height of the dog. His bone and muscle mass must be sufficient to balance his frame, giving a compact and very powerful appearance.

Serious Faults—Lack of proportion, undersized, oversized, reversal of sex characteristics (bitchy dogs, doggy bitches).

Head

Of medium length, broad between the ears; forehead line seen in profile is moderately arched; zygomatic arch and stop well developed with strong broad upper and lower jaws. The desired ratio of backskull to muzzle is 3 to 2. Forehead is preferred dry, however some wrinkling may occur when dog is alert. Expression is noble, alert, and self-assured.

Eyes of medium size, almond shaped with well-fitting lids, moderately deep-set, neither protruding nor receding. The desired color is a uniform dark brown. *Serious Faults*—Yellow (bird of prey) eyes, eyes of different color or size, hairless eye rim. *Disqualification*—Entropion, ectropion.

Ears of medium size, pendant, triangular in shape; when carried alertly, the ears are level with the top of the skull and appear to broaden it. Ears are to be set well apart, hanging forward with the inner edge lying tightly against the head and terminating at approximately mid-cheek. **Serious Faults**—Improper carriage (creased, folded, or held away from cheek/head).

Muzzle—Bridge is straight, broad at base with slight tapering towards tip. The end of the muzzle is broad with well developed chin. Nose is broad rather than round and always black.

Lips—Always black; corners closed; inner mouth pigment is preferred dark. **Serious Faults**—Total lack of mouth pigment (pink mouth).

Bite and Dentition—Teeth 42 in number (20 upper, 22 lower), strong, correctly placed, meeting in a scissors bite, lower incisors touching inside of upper incisors. **Serious Faults**—Level bite; any missing tooth. **Disqualifications**—Overshot, undershot (when incisors do not touch or mesh); wry mouth; two or more missing teeth.

Neck, Topline, Body

Neck—Powerful, well muscled, moderately long, slightly arched and without loose skin. Topline—The back is firm and level, extending in a straight line from behind the withers to the croup. The back remains horizontal to the ground while the dog is moving or standing. Body—The chest is roomy, broad and deep, reaching to elbow, with well pronounced forechest and well sprung, oval ribs. Back is straight and strong. Loin is short, deep, and well muscled. Croup is broad, of medium length, and only slightly sloping. Underline of a mature Rottweiler has a slight tuck-up. Males must have two normal testicles properly descended into the scrotum. **Disqualification**—Unilateral cryptorchid or cryptorchid males. Tail—Tail docked short, close to body, leaving one or two tail vertebrae. The set of the tail is more important than length. Properly set, it gives an impression of elongation of topline; carried slightly above horizontal when the dog is excited or moving.

Forequarters

Shoulder blade is long and well laid back. Upper arm equal in length to shoulder blade, set so elbows are well under body. Distance from withers to elbow and elbow to ground is equal. Legs are strongly developed with straight, heavy bone, not set close together. Pasterns are strong, springy, and almost perpendicular to the ground. Feet are round, compact with well arched toes, turning neither in nor out. Pads are thick and hard. Nails short, strong, and black. Dewclaws may be removed.

Hindquarters

Angulation of hindquarters balances that of forequarters. Upper thigh is fairly long, very broad, and well muscled. Stifle joint is well turned. Lower thigh is long, broad, and powerful, with extensive muscling leading into a strong hock joint. Rear pasterns are nearly perpendicular to the ground. Viewed from the rear, hind legs are straight, strong, and wide enough apart to fit with a properly built body. Feet are somewhat longer than the front feet, turning neither in nor out, equally compact with well arched toes. Pads are thick and hard. Nails short, strong, and black. Dewclaws must be removed.

Coat

Outer coat is straight, coarse, dense, of medium length, and lying flat. Undercoat should be present on neck and thighs, but the amount is influenced by climatic conditions. Undercoat should not show through outer coat. The coat is shortest on head, ears, and legs, longest on breeching. The Rottweiler is to be exhibited in the natural condition with no trimming. *Fault*–Wavy coat. *Serious Faults*– Open, excessively short, or curly coat; total lack of undercoat; any trimming that alters the length of the natural coat. *Disqualification*– Long coat.

Color

Always black with rust to mahogany markings. The demarcation between black and rust is to be clearly defined. The markings should be located as follows: a spot over each eye; on cheeks; as a strip around each side of muzzle, but not on the bridge of the nose; on throat; triangular mark on both sides of prosternum; on forelegs from carpus downward to the toes; on inside of rear legs showing down the front of the stifle and broadening out to front of rear legs from hock to toes, but not completely eliminating black from rear of pasterns; under tail; black penciling on toes. The undercoat is gray, tan, or black. Quantity and location of rust markings is important and should not exceed ten percent of body color. *Serious Faults*—Straw-colored, excessive, insufficient, or sooty markings; rust marking other than described above; white marking any place on dog (a few rust or white hairs do not constitute a marking). *Disqualifications*—Any base color other than black; absence of all markings.

Gait

The Rottweiler is a trotter. His movement should be balanced, harmonious, sure, powerful, and unhindered, with strong forereach and a powerful rear drive. The motion is effortless, efficient, and ground-covering. Front and rear legs are thrown neither in nor out, as the imprint of hind feet should touch that of forefeet. In a trot the forequarters and hindquarters are mutually coordinated while the back remains level, firm, and relatively motionless. As speed increases the legs will converge under body towards a center line.

Temperament

The Rottweiler is basically a calm, confident, and courageous dog with a self-assured aloofness that does not lend itself to immediate and indiscriminate friendships. A Rottweiler is self-confident and responds quietly and with a wait-and-see attitude to influences in his environment. He has an inherent desire to protect home and family and is an intelligent dog of extreme hardness and adaptability with a strong willingness to work, making him especially suited as a companion, guardian, and general all-purpose dog.

The behavior of the Rottweiler in the show ring should be controlled, willing, and adaptable, trained to submit to examination of mouth, testicles, etc. An aloof or reserved dog should not be penalized, as this reflects the accepted character of the breed. An aggressive or belligerent attitude towards other dogs should not be faulted.

A judge shall excuse from the ring any shy Rottweiler. A dog shall be judged fundamentally shy if, refusing to stand for examination, it shrinks away from the judge. A dog that in the opinion of the judge menaces or threatens him/her, or exhibits any sign that it may not be safely approached or examined by the judge in the normal manner, shall be excused from the ring. A dog that in the opinion of the judge attacks any person in the ring shall be disqualified.

Summary

Faults—The foregoing is a description of the ideal Rottweiler. Any structural fault that detracts from the above described working dog must be penalized to the extent of the deviation.

Disqualifications

Entropion, ectropion. Overshot, undershot (when incisors do not touch or mesh); wry mouth; two or more missing teeth. Unilateral cryptorchid or cryptorchid males. Long coat. Any base color other than black; absence of all markings. A dog that in the opinion of the judge attacks any person in the ring.

Approved May 8, 1990
Effective June 28, 1990

Interpretation of the Rottweiler Standard

Now that you've read the rottweiler standard, perhaps you're wondering what it means. When reading a standard, you must interpret what the standard means. Some interpretations are quantitative, meaning that you can define it due to a number, but many interpretations are subjective.

 **Alert!**

When you read over this interpretation, you should understand that this is the author's interpretation of the standard and not necessarily the interpretation that a certain breeder or American Rottweiler Club might have.

General Appearance

In "General Appearance," the rottweiler is defined as a large dog, not as big as some of the giant breeds (St. Bernards, Newfoundlands, etc.), but still bigger than dogs that may be defined as large (boxers, Samoyeds). Males are heavier boned than females and look masculine. Females look feminine. Rotties are black with rust-colored markings—anything else is unacceptable.

Size, Proportion, Substance

Male rotties are 24 to 27 inches when measured at the shoulders. Female rotties are 22 to 25 inches at the shoulder. It is preferable for males to be about 25½ inches at the shoulder and for females to be about 23½ inches at the shoulder. When looking at a rottie lengthwise to heightwise, the dog should be almost square. His height should be nine-tenths of his length. For example, if you measured a 25-inch-tall male rottweiler's body length (just the body, not the head or tail), it should be almost 28 inches long. On that same dog, the rottie's chest should be about 12½ inches from the top of his back to the deepest point of his chest.

A fault (that is, something that is penalized in the show ring) is a dog that doesn't measure up to these proportions, or a male dog that looks feminine or a female dog that looks masculine.

Head

A rottie should have a strong, powerful head with broad jaws. His head (without the muzzle) should be about twice the length of the dog's entire muzzle. The forehead should not have wrinkles except when the dog looks alert.

The rottweiler's eyes should be dark brown and almond-shaped. Dogs with light-colored eyes, eyes of different color other than dark brown, or without hair under the brow are severely penalized in conformation shows. Dogs that have diseases of the eyelid (entropion, ectropion) are disqualified.

 **Fact**

Rottie ears should look like they're alert and should be triangular. The ear should be no longer than mid-cheek. Ears that are too long, too short, or have extra folds in them are faults in the show ring.

A rottie's muzzle and nose are broad. The muzzle has no dips or bumps in it—instead it should be straight. Nose and lips must be black or it is a serious fault. Rottweilers must have forty-two teeth. Having a missing tooth is a fault; having two or more missing teeth disqualifies the dog from the show ring.

The correct bite (that is, how the teeth fit together) is a scissors bite. This means that the upper front teeth fit snugly just in front of the lower front teeth when your rottie closes his mouth. Level bite (where the upper front teeth and the lower front teeth touch edge to edge) is a fault, and any other bite is a disqualification.

Neck, Topline, Body

The rottweiler has a powerful body with a straight back, neither sloping nor having any apparent curve. His skin doesn't have wrinkles anywhere. His chest is very powerful and oval-shaped. His rear may slope slightly to the tail, which must be docked. A male that has one or both undescended testicles is disqualified from the show ring.

▲ The rottweiler's appearance should conform to the breed standard.

Forequarters and Hindquarters

On the front legs, shoulders are powerful and set at the correct angle. The distance from the top of the shoulder to the elbow should be the same as the distance from the elbow to the ground. Legs should be muscular, and feet should be compact so that they look round if you drew an outline around them. Feet should be straight when the dog stands. Toenails should be black. Dewclaws can be removed.

 **Question?**

What are dewclaws?
Dewclaws are the bumps with nails you find on the back of a dog's leg a little way up from its foot. While they may have had a specific importance during the evolution of the dog, today they do not serve any particular function.

Hindquarters are powerful and angular, and should balance the forequarters. The back paws are slightly bigger than the front paws, still round, and should be straight when the dog stands. Toenails should be black. Dewclaws must be removed.

Coat and Color

Coat should be coarse, dense, and medium length with an undercoat. Serious faults include a wavy, soft, curly, or short coat. Absence of an undercoat is also a fault. Long coat is a disqualification.

▲ According to the standard, rottweilers should always be black with rust to mahogany markings.

The rottie must be black with rust-colored markings in the following places:

- Dots over the eyes and on the cheeks.
- Stripe on each side of the muzzle.
- On throat.
- Two triangles on each side of the sternum.
- On the forelegs from the wrists to the toes.

- On the underside of the dog.
- From hock to toes on the back legs.

The undercoat is gray, tan, or black. Any other coloring is either a fault or a disqualification.

Gait and Temperament

Rottweilers are powerful trotters. Any other gait is not acceptable.

Rottweilers are calm and confident. He may be aloof, but will submit to inspection by a judge. Shyness or aggression in the ring isn't permitted, and any dog that attacks a person in the ring is disqualified.

Understand the Rottie Personality

So, now you understand a little more about the rottweiler through the standard, but what does this mean in terms of personality? Rotties are naturally protective dogs. They can be lovable lugs or aloof, but all have a sense of territory. This means that a stranger who enters the yard or house may be considered suspect, whether he is a burglar or the postal carrier. Rottweilers love their families and friends, but they may be hesitant to accept new people.

Rottweiler Aggressiveness and Guarding Instincts

Are rottweilers aggressive? The answer depends on the dog. Yes, there are aggressive rottweilers out there, but most aggressive dogs are the products of puppy mills, backyard breeders, or poor training and socialization. Those dogs that are bred for good temperaments and that are properly trained and socialized make good pets, with some rare exceptions.

The rottweiler personality is loyalty embodied. Rotties can be one-person or one-family dogs. It is in their nature to guard people and things, and they are not happy left alone. They feel most secure with "their person" and are unhappy if "their person" is not around. Rottweilers make poor backyard dogs and should never be chained.

 **Essential**

One thing you should think about is what you are planning to do with the dog. Be honest with yourself (and the breeder) when looking for a rottweiler. If you're looking for just a pet, ask the breeder if her dogs are very active. If you're a laid-back person, a very active puppy may not fit well with your personality.

Because of the breed's natural guarding instincts, rottweiler owners must take care that their dogs are never put in a situation where the dog might think something harmless is a threat to the owner or property. Unless familiar with boisterous hugs and loud greetings, a rottweiler may mistake a joyful greeting for an attack on his owner. Meter readers and lawn-care professionals may avoid a house with a large rottweiler in the backyard because the dog may back them into a corner of the yard and not leave them alone until the owner rescues them.

Naturally, the rottweiler makes a good watchdog and a good guard dog. A well-bred, well-trained, properly socialized rottie is a joy to own. He's a loyal friend and companion that you will love and respect for many years. He can be quietly dignified or a clown to those he loves. Those who own a rottie couldn't imagine owning another breed.

The Perfect Rottweiler Owners

If a rottie could talk, he'd say that the perfect rottweiler owner is someone who doesn't mind being in charge. This person would be a mature adult or perhaps a teenager because a rottie is naturally big and maybe a little clumsy and can knock over small kids or even a lightweight adult.

That owner would understand the need to train the rottweiler with a consistent but gentle hand. The owner would be active, too. After all, rottweilers are working dogs that love having a job to do.

If a rottie gets bored, he'll find something to do that people generally don't like—usually something like chewing, digging, or barking.

 **Alert!**

Rottweilers are generally not good pets for people who cannot handle a large dog. This includes the elderly, children, or persons with disabilities that may limit their strength. In these cases, if you still want a rottweiler, a smaller (typically female), specially trained, or more mature dog with good obedience training may be more appropriate.

If a rottie could speak, he'd tell you he has to be by his owner or with his family all the time. It's very important for him, you see. Being with you makes him feel secure and happy; being alone makes him frightened and nervous. He's very protective and doesn't need training to know what to do if someone threatens his people.

So, owning a rottie is a bit of a challenge. The rottweiler is not an average dog—he is an exceptional dog. Are you feeling up to the task?

The Working Dog

Rottweilers are naturally athletic dogs. Their versatility makes them excellent agility and obedience dogs. Because of their herding backgrounds, rottweilers and Samoyeds are the only dogs not in the Herding Group that are allowed into AKC herding competitions.

Rotties can also earn their Schutzhund titles. Schutzhund was originally developed for German shepherds in Germany. However, it tests the obedience, tracking, and protection ability in any dog, not just German shepherds. Schutzhund is commonly mistaken for attack dog training. While protection is certainly a part of Schutzhund training, Schutzhund also tests the controllability and the working ability of the dog.

▲ Rottweilers make great working dogs—even if they sometimes prefer to let someone else to do the work!

In addition to making great Schutzhund dogs, rottweilers can also earn obedience, agility, herding, and tracking titles through the AKC and the United Kennel Club (UKC). The North American Dog Agility Council (NADAC) and the United States Dog Agility Association (USDAA) also offer agility titles to rottweilers.

 **Fact**

Another activity rottweilers enjoy is carting. When rotties were butcher dogs, they often pulled carts for their masters. The American Rottweiler Club has a special carting division in which your rottie can earn titles carting.

The rottweiler makes an excellent police dog although not quite as popular as other breeds in police work. This may be in part due to their larger size or their intolerance to heat (their black coat makes them especially sensitive to warm days). A large and intelligent dog, the rottweiler has made a good police dog, minding his handler and doing an excellent job in catching criminals.

The Attraction and Downsides to the Rottweiler

Now that you know a bit about rotties from the standard, their personality, and the work they do, let's talk about the rottweiler in general. Rottweilers are great-looking dogs and are impressive, too. If you've ever seen someone walking with a rottie, you'll note he's a dog that instantly commands respect. Rottweilers are powerful dogs, bigger and blockier than the Doberman or German shepherd, because of their mastiff heritage.

But owning a rottweiler can be a bit of a challenge. For one thing, rottweilers are big. Really big. They can accidentally knock over someone if rambunctious or untrained. And they can be very intimidating to those who aren't comfortable around dogs. While this can be a benefit, there are many people who are prejudiced against rottweilers. This can be seen in the breed bans that pop up around the country, which often name rottweilers as dangerous dogs. Owners of rottweilers can be denied liability insurance or forced to pay exorbitant premiums on their homeowners insurance.

 **Essential**

Puppies can be a gamble when it comes to how they'll turn out. This is important if you're looking for a show prospect or a pet with a certain temperament. You can mitigate some of this surprise by purchasing from a reputable breeder who breeds for stable temperaments.

Much of this worry is completely unjustified; however, there is a problem of owners with "big dog machismo." Great dogs such as the rottweiler often attract people who have no business owning a rottweiler. Because rottweilers look tough, some people like to get a rottweiler or two because they think it makes them look tough. The problem is these people don't understand the requirements of dog ownership and quite often, the dogs suffer.

Many rottweilers are loving additions to the family. They're naturally protective of their owners but not necessarily aggressive. When properly socialized, they make great therapy dogs and working dogs.

So, is the rottweiler a good dog or a bad dog to own? That depends a lot on you, your time, knowledge, and commitment to this special breed. In some circumstances, you may decide that the rottweiler would not be an appropriate dog. In other cases, you may find them a loyal, lifelong companion. Ⓔ

CHAPTER 2

Looking for a Rottweiler

YOU'VE THOUGHT ABOUT getting a dog, and getting a rottie appeals to you now that you know a little bit about the breed and its history. But are you ready for dog ownership—in particular, rottie ownership? Owning a rottweiler takes a commitment on the owner's part, and with a rottweiler that typically means a ten- to thirteen-year commitment. Are you willing to take that responsibility? And where do you find the perfect rottweiler? There are plenty of places willing to sell you a rottie, but only a few of those are good sources. Do you know where to look and what to look out for?

Should You Get a Rottweiler?

If you've picked up this book with the intention of learning a bit more about rotties before you purchase one, the first question you must ask yourself is if you should get a dog at all and if that dog should be a rottweiler. When considering whether you would be a good dog owner, consider the following:

- A dog requires food, water, adequate shelter, exercise, and attention every day. Are you able to provide these things?
- Do you have time to exercise and train a large dog?
- Can you afford a dog?
- Are you home often enough to spend time with your dog?

- Do you have a large enough yard with a six-foot fence so your rottweiler can exercise and be safely contained?
- Can you physically handle a large dog?
- Are you able to properly socialize and train a dog with natural protective tendencies to make certain he is not a liability?
- Does everyone in your family want a dog and in particular a rottweiler?
- Do you live where you can own pets?
- Is anyone in the family allergic to dogs?
- Can you deal with the destructiveness of a pet?
- Do you understand the temperament of the rottweiler and what obligations you have in owning one?

These questions are intended to remind you of your responsibility in rottweiler ownership. Rottweilers are large dogs. They must be properly socialized with people and other animals if they are going to be enjoyable to own. Dogs, especially puppies, take time to raise and train. If you don't have the time to spend with a dog, perhaps a rottweiler is not for you.

▲ Depending on the amount of free time you're able to invest in a dog, one rottweiler might be adequate for you and your family.

Kids and Dogs

You may be thinking about getting a dog for the kids. After all, kids and dogs naturally go together. However, before you get a dog for the kids, realize that the dog is your responsibility, not the children's. Children can't be expected to take responsibility for a living thing. Kids are immature and aren't always reliable.

 **Fact**

Dogs mean a big investment in time and money. The purchase price of a dog doesn't include vet visits, deworming, vaccinations, heartworm pills, dog food, toys, and various supplies. Nor does it take into account the amount of time you must spend with the dog. If you're gone a lot, you may want to reconsider getting a dog.

This doesn't mean that your children can't learn from owning a pet. You can have your children feed your rottie and give him water—under your supervision. They can play and enjoy your rottie while you watch. Never leave a young child alone with any dog.

Where to Look for Your Rottweiler

You've made up your mind that you want a dog, and you've determined that a rottie might be the dog for you. But where do you obtain a rottweiler? Reputable breeders, animal shelters, and rescue organizations are all valid places to look for your rottie. We'll look at each of them below.

When people think about getting a dog, the first thing that comes to mind may be a pet store. After all, you get groceries at a grocery store and gas at a gas station, so why not get a pet at a pet store? Well, going to the store is great if you're buying bananas but not if you're buying a dog. You're looking for a ten-plus-year companion, not a bunch of fruit. Not all dogs are the same or of the same quality, even though they may be priced and appear the same. Treating a dog like a disposable item is what helps contribute to the pet overpopulation and is part of the reason that millions of pets are euthanized in shelters every year. Let's look at the reputable breeder and why you may want to buy your rottie from one.

Reputable Breeders

What exactly is a reputable breeder? A reputable breeder is someone who seeks to improve the rottweiler breed. He or she isn't breeding dogs to make a quick buck but to produce the finest rottweilers for conformation or performance work. Reputable breeders choose their dogs carefully when they breed. Their dogs are screened for genetic diseases, and they offer guarantees they back up with a contract.

The reputable breeder's dogs have conformation or performance titles on them. The breeder will be glad to tell you everything about your puppy's ancestry—in fact, you're likely to get inundated with photographs of dogs when you ask about them. If one of the parents isn't a champion, the breeder is working toward obtaining a championship. When you're done talking to the reputable breeder, you know her dogs are her kids.

 **Question?**

How much do rottweilers cost?
A show-quality rottweiler can cost $800 to $1,000 or more.
A pet-quality rottweiler should cost between $400 and $800.

Puppies are not always available, and the reputable breeder often has a waiting list. Seldom does a reputable breeder breed more than two litters a year. A reputable breeder screens the buyer to make certain that the buyer will provide a good home for the rottweiler and that the rottweiler is the right dog for the buyer.

When you buy a rottweiler puppy from a reputable breeder, the breeder doesn't stop caring about the puppy he or she sold you. Reputable breeders like to hear back from puppy buyers and are happy to be a resource for further information. You can ask your reputable breeder about veterinarians in your area, advice on housebreaking your rottie, and other questions you might have.

Animal Shelters

Another place to look for your rottweiler is the animal shelter or "pound." Surprisingly, a quarter of all dogs that appear in an animal shelter are purebreds. Because rottweilers are popular, you may find both purebreds and rottweiler mixes in the animal shelter. Most rottweilers you find at the shelter will be adolescents and adults. Occasionally, you may find puppies, but this is not as common.

People give up their dogs at the shelter for a number of reasons. In some cases, behavior may have a role in it. In other cases, the former owner may not have realized what a responsibility owning a dog is. Still other dogs are strays or had owners who died or had to give them up. Whatever the reason, you should ask the shelter about the known history of the dog.

 Fact

Animal shelters and breed rescues are a cheaper alternative to purchasing a dog from a breeder. The shelter or rescue will still charge a fee, but it is often less than what you would pay if you bought a puppy from a breeder. If you are looking for a companion and not a show dog, this is a viable alternative.

When you rescue a dog from a shelter, you usually don't know the dog's history or pedigree. Dogs coming from shelters are usually pet quality and must be spayed or neutered. However, if you are planning on your rottie to be just a pet or to compete in performance competitions (obedience, tracking, herding, agility, and Schutzhund), this shouldn't be a concern. You'll be getting a pet and saving a life.

Rescue Organizations

Another place to look for rottweilers is a rottweiler or purebred rescue organization. These rescue organizations are usually affiliated with a breed club such as the American Rottweiler Club. Rescue workers are volunteers who usually screen the buyer to make certain he or she is a good match for the rottie.

▲ Rottweilers make wonderful family pets.

You may find rotties from reputable breeders that need new homes, or you may find rotties rescued from shelters or from situations where the owner could not keep the dog. Dogs may be of any age, but you're more likely to see adolescents and adults rather than puppies. The American Rottweiler Club has its own breed rescue. Contact the National Breed Rescue for a breed rescue in your area (see Appendix A).

Where Not to Look for Your Rottweiler and Why

There are other places you could purchase your rottweiler, but these are generally not good places to look. These include backyard breeders, puppy mills, and pet stores. Let's take a look at each of these sources for puppies.

Backyard Breeders

Backyard breeders are usually people who just recently got into breeding dogs. They have a purebred bitch, and they think that breeding their rottweiler will make them money, so they breed with the first available stud. Their rottie may or may not be AKC registered and is most likely a pet-quality dog from a pet shop or another backyard breeder. The owner doesn't know the history of the dog and doesn't have any titles on her.

 Alert!

> No matter how cute, don't buy that puppy in the window! Pet shops often purchase dogs from commercial breeders or puppy mills. These puppies often have no certifications against hereditary diseases and many are poorly socialized.

At first, it may seem convenient to buy from a local backyard breeder. After all, you just want a pet, right? The problem is that backyard breeders don't screen for hip dysplasia, cardiac problems, or other genetic ailments. They don't understand the AKC standard and are likely to produce substandard dogs. They won't offer temperament testing, a contract, or a guarantee if something goes wrong. What's more, buying a puppy from backyard breeders only encourages them to breed their dog to make more money. Their dogs often sadly end up in shelters or in rescue. If they can't sell their puppies, they may dump the puppies in the shelter. Do you want to encourage that?

Puppy Mills

Another type of breeder is the puppy mill. The puppy mill, as its name suggests, churns out puppies for sale. Puppies are always available. They may breed several breeds or may breed only one breed.

A puppy mill might seem like a good place to get a rottweiler puppy, especially if you're in a hurry. But, think about where you're buying your puppy from. Like the backyard breeder, the puppy mill is in this to make money. That means no genetic screening, no selective breeding, and no temperament testing. There are no guarantees, or if there are, they are usually fraught with unusual clauses designed to give the puppy mill a way not to honor them. But, it gets worse than that.

Many puppy mills are overcrowded, and the pups are raised in squalid conditions with little or no socializing. The parents of the puppies are kept strictly to breed and are condemned to a terrible existence. Every year, there are raids on puppy mills where dogs are rescued from abominable conditions. Inevitably, many are very sick and have to be euthanized. While not all puppy mills are like this, many are. Do you want to encourage this practice?

 Alert!

Run, don't walk, from anyone who tries to pressure you into buying a rottweiler puppy. The sense of urgency on the breeder's part is definitely not something a responsible breeder would display to a potential buyer. A responsible breeder wants to make sure that the match is a good fit and that her puppy won't come back, or worse, end up in a shelter or rescue.

Pet Shops

What about pet shops? Well, reputable breeders don't sell their dogs to pet shops because they have no control over who is buying their puppies. Reputable breeders want to make certain that the home they sell a puppy to is the right home. How are they able to do this if they never speak to the buyer? Pet shops are in the business of selling a pet. That means the dog goes to whoever hands them the purchase price. If you go into a pet store and ask about health certifications, it is unlikely they'd have any to show you. What's worse is that most pet shops buy from commercial breeders and puppy mills. Do you want to support that industry? The only place to look for your rottweiler besides a shelter or rescue is at the home of a reputable breeder.

Health Certificates and Common Hereditary Diseases

Before you look for a reputable breeder, you need to learn about health certificates and hereditary diseases that are common to the rottweiler. Because of their popularity in the 1980s, the rottweiler has suffered from overbreeding at the hands of puppy mills and backyard breeders. As a result, the rottweiler has a number of genetic diseases that the breeder should screen for. These include, but are not limited to, the following:

- Hip dysplasia
- Elbow dysplasia and osteochrondrosis dissecans (OCD)
- Eye problems
- Heart problems
- Von Willebrand's disease (canine hemophilia)

Don't believe breeders if they say that their dogs don't have hip dysplasia or elbow dysplasia. Ask for proof. The only way a dog can be proven not to have hip dysplasia or elbow dysplasia is through an x-ray read by a professional.

A reputable breeder will furnish proof of tests that the parents of the puppies were screened for certain genetic diseases. There are several registries that can provide this proof, including the Orthopedic Foundation for Animals (OFA), PennHIP, and Canine Eye Registry Foundation (CERF).

Health Registries

OFA is perhaps the best known of the registries that does genetic registration for hip dysplasia, elbow dysplasia, heart conditions, thyroid, and other potential genetic problems. OFA is simply a registry that ranks the tests (x-rays, labwork, and so on) and keeps the results in a database. Their Web site is *www.offa.org*.

PennHIP is a relatively new registry. It is concerned with primarily orthopedic issues such as hips and elbows. Their Web site is *www.synbiotics.com*.

CERF is affiliated with Purdue University. A local veterinarian (in this case, a veterinary ophthalmologist) does the eye exam and reports the results to CERF. The Web site for CERF is *www.vet.purdue.edu/~yshen/cerf.html/*. (See Appendix A for OFA, PennHIP, and CERF addresses and phone numbers.)

Hip Dysplasia

Hip dysplasia is a crippling genetic condition in which the hip's ball and socket are malformed. Hip dysplasia can be mild to severe. In milder cases, anti-inflammatories and "nutriceuticals" (supplements that are classified as food by the FDA but appear to have some medicinal properties) may help mitigate it, but in medium to severe cases, expensive surgery may be needed to correct it. Hip dysplasia is very painful, and some dogs that suffer from it may have to be euthanized.

 Fact

Hip dysplasia is common in rottweilers. The OFA shows that nearly 21 percent of those rottweilers registered had some form of hip dysplasia, making this the twenty-fifth worst breed for hip dysplasia.

Don't accept the breeder's word that the puppy is clear of hip dysplasia or that hip dysplasia doesn't run in his dogs' lines. You can't tell if a dog has hip dysplasia by looking. The only way to tell is through an x-ray. Ask the breeder to show you the certificates that prove that the puppy's parents have been cleared of hip dysplasia.

Both OFA and PennHIP provide registries for dogs. The OFA gives the following ratings for hips: excellent, good, fair, and poor. Poor is indicative of hip dysplasia. A breeder should not breed a dog with a rating less than "good." The OFA certificate is printed on blue paper. Always ask to see the original certificate, as some disreputable breeders have been known to photocopy the certificates and change the names on them. You can also look up the dogs' ratings online at ✑www.offa.org to confirm their certification. You will need either the parents' AKC numbers or registered names (full or part) to look them up in the OFA database.

Elbow Dysplasia

Another common ailment among rottweilers is elbow dysplasia. There are three types of recognized elbow dysplasia, which has a number of hereditary and environmental factors. Rottweilers are the second worst breed for the disease, with the OFA showing that nearly 42 percent of those registered are dysplastic. As with hip dysplasia, the number is no doubt higher given that registrations are voluntary.

Elbow dysplasia may require expensive surgery to correct. One form of elbow dysplasia, OCD, is very painful and will need surgery. Again, don't accept the breeder's word that elbow dysplasia doesn't run in his or her lines or that the parents don't have it. Ask for proof through either PennHIP or OFA certificates, or look up the dogs' names (full or partial) or AKC registration number at ✑www.offa.org.

Eye Diseases

Rottweilers suffer from a variety of genetic eye ailments that can lead to blindness. Some, like entropion and ectropion, cause severe discomfort because the eyelashes rub against the dog's eyes, and these require surgery to correct. CERF has a certification that is good for one year. It certifies that the dog's parents were clear of eye diseases at the time of breeding.

 **Essenᵗial**

Eye problems can occur at any time. Some, like entropion, the puppy is born with, but others, such as PRA (progressive retinal atrophy) may appear later. This is why it's important for the parents to be certified yearly.

The CERF certification is pass or fail. Ask to see the original certificate. You can also search for the dog's CERF certification on the CERF Web site at ✑*www.vmdb.org* and search with the dog's name (full or partial) or AKC registration number.

Heart Problems

Rottweilers suffer from a number of heart problems, including a malformation of the heart vessels known as subaortic stenosis (SAS). OFA has a cardiac registry, but like many newer registries, few breeders know about it. As of December 2002, fewer than 1,500 dogs had been registered. Given the popularity of rottweilers, we don't have accurate statistics on how many actually have cardiac problems.

Since SAS is nearly always fatal, it is a good idea to find a breeder who does register his or her dogs with the OFA cardiac database. Like the other OFA databases, this is searchable by a dog's registered name or AKC registration number.

Von Willebrand's Disease

Von Willebrand's disease (VWD) is a bleeding disorder in dogs similar to hemophilia. There are three types of VWD. Rottweilers suffer from Type I VWD. While the breeder should have both of your prospective rottweiler's parents tested for VWD with a simple blood test, there is no genetic test to determine Type I VWD carriers in rottweilers. A company called Vetgen has developed a test for Bernese Mountain Dogs, so maybe in the future there will be a test for rottweilers as well.

 **Fact**

Even if you purchase your rottweiler from a reputable breeder, there is still a chance that your rottie may have a genetic condition, despite the testing. This is why it's very important to buy from a breeder who is willing to replace or refund the puppy.

Locating a Reputable Breeder

You now know things to look out for when searching for a rottweiler. You're searching for a breeder who will screen for genetic diseases, be choosy about which dogs she breeds so that she produces the very best, and will guarantee her dogs—that is, will replace or refund the price of the dog if a genetic health problem occurs and will take back a dog under any circumstance.

Questions to Ask a Reputable Breeder

But where do you find such a breeder? As you may guess, you're not likely to find them in classified ads, although occasionally you might. Contact the American Rottweiler Club for a referral list of those breeders in your area.

But your job isn't done yet. Contact a few breeders in your area and ask if they're planning on breeding a litter any time soon. You should then ask questions to determine if the breeder is a responsible or reputable breeder.

1. How long have you been interested in rottweilers?
2. How long have you been breeding rottweilers?
3. Do you show (or participate in performance events with)

your rottweilers? Are you affiliated with any local or national clubs?

4. What titles do your dogs have? With what organizations?
5. Why did you choose to breed these two rottweilers? Do you breed for show, work, or performance?
6. What can you tell me about their ancestry and what makes them suitable to breed?
7. How many litters do you produce each year?
8. Do you screen for genetic diseases? Which ones? Can you show me the original certificates?
9. Are your dogs AKC registered? Can you show me the papers?
10. Do you have a contract? May I see the contract? Do you offer guarantees for hips, eyes, etc.?
11. May I have a tour of your kennel and meet you and your dogs?
12. Can you provide references?

If the breeder isn't put off by your questions and is willing to answer, you may have found a reputable breeder. Reputable breeders like talking to informed puppy buyers and will be happy to answer any of your questions. If the breeder on the other end of the line acts affronted, look for your puppy somewhere else!

When you visit a reputable breeder, you should be able to meet with any of the dogs there (with a proper introduction). The kennels should be well maintained, and you should feel comfortable meeting with the dogs and the breeder. Keep in mind, though, that if there are puppies, it is natural for the female rottweiler to be protective of them.

A reputable breeder will not pressure you into buying a puppy right there. The breeder may want to meet your entire family to see how they react to rottweilers. Don't forget, these are big dogs and require a certain amount of responsibility.

CHAPTER 3

Choosing a Rottweiler

NOW THAT YOU KNOW where to look for a rottweiler, your next step is to decide what type of rottweiler to get. Not all rotties are alike! You need to know how to pick the right rottie for you and your family. You'll also need to know about registrations and papers. Do you know the difference between the contract, registration, and pedigree? If not, then you'll soon learn.

Your Rottweiler Choices

Now you have some choices to make. Some are easy; some are tough. Do you want a puppy or an adult? A male rottie or a female? Working or show lines? You need to understand the differences so you can find the rottie that will suit your lifestyle.

Puppy or Adult?

Most people think about getting a puppy when they think about getting a dog. While getting a puppy has its merits, don't overlook an adolescent or adult rottie. You should consider all options when trying to decide which rottweiler is right for you.

Puppies are adorable, there's no doubt about it. Rottie pups are so cute that it is hard to resist one. But before you purchase that oh-so-adorable wiggly ball of joy, think about whether you have the time to invest in a puppy. A puppy is a clean slate but needs the proper training and socialization to become a well-trained rottweiler. Puppies are time-consuming—they require constant attention, training, and socialization. They aren't housetrained either; something you may want to think about if you've just installed new carpet.

 **Fact**

Most people have the mistaken notion that puppies bond better than adult dogs. While it may take a little longer (a few days instead of hours), adult dogs often bond as well as puppies in a relatively short time.

Many adult rottweilers are housebroken already or can be housetrained easily. Some adult rotties may know a few commands. Adults usually need less attention than younger dogs and may not need as much activity. Both adults and puppies may be destructive, though adults are usually less so since they are not teething.

So which is better? It depends a lot on the time you have. Puppies bond quickly to new owners, but most adult rotties will also bond, though it may take a little longer. Adult rotties may have learned some bad habits from previous owners that you may have to break, but then, you can also cause bad habits in new pups. You can't leave a puppy alone for more than four hours when he is younger than six months; an older dog can wait for nine hours if necessary.

Be honest with yourself. Do you have the time for a puppy? If you do, then great! Otherwise, consider an adult or adolescent rottweiler.

Male or Female?

Male or female? For the most part, it is a matter of personal preference. Male rotties tend to be bigger and may have dominance issues. Female rottweilers are smaller than males and tend to be less concerned with dominance. A first-time dog owner may want to consider a female rottweiler because she may be apt to be more trainable.

◀ Owning multiple rottweilers can be a rewarding experience for you and your dogs—who are sure to enjoy the extra company.

However, if you do not spay a female rottweiler, she will go into season, or estrus, twice a year. This can last from two to four weeks and will attract male dogs during this time. You must make certain that your intact female rottweiler stays safely away from potential suitors.

Male rottweilers can be more aggressive than female rottweilers, but female rottweilers can also be aggressive, especially when meeting another dog of the same sex. While aggression between a male and female is uncommon, it can and does occur. If you have a dog that is aggressive toward other dogs, getting a dog of the opposite sex doesn't guarantee that he or she will get along with your new rottweiler.

Considerations with Other Pets

Rottweilers can be aggressive toward other dogs. If you already have another dog, hopefully your other dog is about the same size as a rottweiler. If your dog is much smaller, you may wish to reconsider your choice of breed. Even so, if you plan on getting a rottie as a puppy, he or she can learn to become good friends with the current dog. Regardless, it is a good idea to choose a rottie of the opposite sex as the dog you currently have. This will help reduce aggression.

 Alert!

You may be thinking that two rotties are twice the fun. However, they're about ten times the work. Yes, they keep each other company, but they're also eight paws of trouble. Often siblings will egg each other on into bad behavior. You're also dealing with pack issues when you have two. Unless you're used to having two dogs, try one first.

Rotties can get along with cats, provided they are raised with them as puppies. Most cats swat a curious puppy once or twice and convince the puppy that there are more interesting things to do besides pester a cat. Adult rottweilers may or may not accept a cat. Some rottweilers have enough of a prey drive that they will chase a cat. As a rule, it is best never to leave a cat alone with your rottweiler. You should also keep other pets (birds, rodents, lizards, and so on) out of reach of your rottie.

Considerations with Children

Regardless of what dog breed you own, you should never allow a small child to play with a dog unsupervised. Even the gentlest dog may bite if the child causes that dog pain. If you have several small children, you may wish to wait until they are a little older so that a rottweiler is not too big or intimidating for them.

An enthusiastic rottie can knock over a toddler or even a small child without intending to.

Having one small child is a lot of work. Having a small child and a puppy is like having two babies to care for at once. You may wish to reconsider your desire for a puppy until after your life becomes a little less hectic.

 **Essential**

Did you know that dog ownership actually reduces allergies in children? New studies suggest that owning cats and dogs may actually help allergy-prone children build up a resistance to allergies.

As stated in the previous chapter, children can't be expected to care for a dog properly. Children are children after all, and an adult needs to be responsible for the dog. This doesn't mean that the children can't help you with caring for the dog, but you can't realistically expect a five- or six-year-old to remember that it is time to feed the dog or know when to take the puppy outside to relieve himself.

Rottweilers make great pets for adults, older children, and teenagers, provided that those who will take care of the rottweiler are mature enough to do so.

Age to Bring a Puppy Home

There's been much debate on the best time to take a puppy home. Most breeders and pet professionals agree that you shouldn't take a puppy away from his mother before 7½ weeks. Most breeders will insist on keeping the puppy until eight or nine weeks old, and many municipalities forbid the sale of puppies younger than eight weeks.

What's so important about eight weeks, and why must the puppy stay with his mother and siblings so long? Much of this has to do with socialization. A puppy needs the security of his mother and his littermates. From the time the puppy is born to the time he leaves his family to join yours, he is learning crucial skills. He is learning to become a dog. His interaction with his mother and siblings teach him the proper way to behave around other dogs.

If you take a puppy away from his family too early, he may develop emotional problems that will plague him the rest of his life. Puppies taken away from their moms at five or six weeks tend to be insecure.

 **Fact**

There's a lot of talk about a "fear period" for puppies. This is when the puppy goes through nervousness or shyness because of new things. Chances are, your puppy may be shy of new things at various times or may not show shyness at all, depending on his personality and his socialization.

At eight weeks, the puppy has been weaned for a few weeks and has had a chance to interact with his mom and siblings full-time. He is still young enough that his behaviors aren't fully set. He has had at least his first set of vaccinations and has possibly been dewormed. Ask the breeder what vaccinations and health care the puppy has had. Don't be overeager to get him before that time. You will have him to enjoy the rest of his life.

Can you get a puppy older than eight weeks? Most certainly! If the puppy is older than eight weeks, he is simply more mature. He will bond readily to you.

Choosing a Puppy

So, now that you've decided you want a puppy, you may wonder how to select the right rottie puppy for you. As you might guess, not all rottweiler puppies have the same personality. Some puppies will be more bossy than others. Some puppies are timid.

If you have found a reputable breeder, that breeder may select a puppy according to what she has learned about you and your situation. The breeder has had eight weeks to evaluate the various temperaments as opposed to you, who will only have a few minutes or an hour at best to see and judge each puppy.

▲ Even from a young age, the markings on rottweilers are easily defined.

If the breeder does not choose a puppy for you or if you have to make a choice between two puppies, you must first decide what type of personality you are looking for. Most pet owners are looking for an easy-going, tractable dog that isn't too difficult to get along with. In puppies, that relates to a puppy that isn't too dominant or aggressive. Dominant puppies are often the first to come to you. They may play more roughly than the other puppies, pinning their siblings or roughhousing with other, more dominant pups.

You also may not want one who is too independent. An independent puppy will show little or no interest in humans, preferring instead to do his own thing. Independent puppies may not care if they please you or not.

 Essential

Having the breeder choose a dog for you is actually better than you choosing your own puppy. While it's exciting to choose for yourself, often people choose a puppy because "he picked me!" Those who "pick" their owners are quite often dominant.

Another type of puppy to look out for is the overly submissive or fearful puppy. This puppy may see you and cower or crouch submissively. When you pet him, his eyes become very wide and he may become very frightened. You don't want a puppy like this because he can turn into a fear-biter.

Temperament Testing

Looks aren't everything when it comes to choosing a pet. You'll need to ask the breeder if you can perform some simple temperament tests to make sure you are getting a dog that will mesh with your personality. You may wish to suggest that the breeder relocate the puppies' mother in case she is very protective of the pups.

Observe the puppies playing. Is there one that is pushy or aggressive? This may be a more dominant puppy. An independent puppy may do things on his own. A submissive puppy may play with other puppies but will look like he's being picked on.

Call the puppies to you. Kneel down and clap your hands. The puppies should look at you curiously and come to you. Any that cringe, run away, or ignore you are probably not a personality you want. (It is okay if the puppy starts coming and suddenly gets distracted or if the puppy comes and then leaves.) With the breeder's permission, pick up and cuddle each of the puppies. A normal reaction to being held and cuddled individually is a little apprehension followed by cheerful acceptance.

Gently turn a puppy over onto his back. If he struggles and fusses violently, let him up. This is a very dominant puppy and one you may not want. If he lies there, submissively urinates, or looks frightened, he is most likely very submissive and may become a fear-biter. One who struggles a bit and then accepts a nice tummy rub is a dog with a personality somewhere in between.

Your rottweiler puppy should show interest in you. Throwing a ball should incite inquisitive play. If the puppy seems lethargic (and hasn't just woken up from a nap) or if something seems wrong, trust your instincts and look for another breeder.

 Question?

When do I want a dominant puppy?
There are times when someone wants a dominant puppy. If you're looking for a strong Schutzhund candidate or a confident conformation dog, a dominant dog may work for you. But you must know how to handle these self-assured rotties, or you may end up with a bully on your hands.

Choosing an Adult

The adult rottweiler should be outgoing and friendly. Avoid any timid or aggressive rottweilers. The rottie may be exuberant, but he should not be hyper when he greets you. If you can, walk the rottie on a leash and spend some time getting to know him. If the rottie knows commands, practice some commands after he has settled down. Offer him a dog biscuit whenever he performs the command correctly.

Spend as much time as you can with your prospective adult rottweiler to decide if this is the one for you. Learn what you can about the adult rottweiler's history. You won't learn everything about the rottweiler in a brief ten-minute session, but you will get a feel for his personality.

What Are Papers?

If you are getting your rottweiler from a breeder, you should receive "papers," or proof of registration. These papers should come from the American Kennel Club (AKC) or the United Kennel Club (UKC). Occasionally, you will find a dog registered with a German or foreign registry such as the Fédération Cynologique Internationale (FCI).

These papers are proof that your rottweiler is a registered purebred. It is not a bill of sale. It doesn't mean your purebred is any more valuable than any other dog. It isn't a symbol of quality. It isn't a guarantee of health.

 Essential

One of the benefits to registering your dog with the AKC is that you will receive a number of free goodies, including a magazine subscription, free treats in the mail, and even free pet health insurance for six months.

Types of AKC Registration

There are three types of AKC registration:

1. **Full registration.** This states the dog may be bred and is eligible to compete in all AKC conformation and performance events.
2. **Limited registration.** This states the dog may not be bred and can't compete in AKC conformation events but may compete in performance events.
3. **Indefinite listing privilege.** This is for dogs with an unknown pedigree that are still obviously purebred. The dog must be spayed or neutered and can't compete in AKC conformation events but may compete in performance events.

Registering Your Rottweiler

Breeders often refer to puppy papers as "blue slips" because for a long time they were small slips of blue paper. Now they're full-size forms. You must fill out this registration and mail it in along with the AKC's fee to register your dog with the AKC. Your rottweiler puppy will not be registered otherwise. Likewise, if you do not complete the change of ownership on the back of a registered dog's papers, you will not be that dog's owner in the eyes of the AKC.

Don't confuse the dog's pedigree with his registration. A pedigree is a family tree. It may have an impressive AKC seal stamped on it, but it doesn't mean your dog is registered with the AKC. You must either have registration papers with the appropriate change of ownership form filled out on the back, or you must have puppy registration papers.

Limited Registration for Pet-Quality Dogs

If you are purchasing a puppy from a reputable breeder, and the breeder decides that the puppy is pet quality, there is a check box that the breeder may check, marking this puppy as a limited registration. Limited registration allows the rottweiler to compete in all performance competitions, but he can't compete in conformation, nor can any of his offspring registered with the AKC. Only the breeder can rescind this limitation in writing.

 Essential

If you haven't neutered him, and your rottie proves to be show quality and you wish to show him in conformation, you can request that the breeder rescind the restriction in writing.

Why would the breeder do this? If the breeder is reputable and has sold your puppy as a pet-quality puppy, she doesn't intend for this puppy to be bred. In fact, she would charge you *more* for a show potential dog. This protects the breeder's reputation by eliminating the possibility of having her buyers turn into backyard breeders, who in turn might register a substandard litter with the AKC.

Registering Shelter or Rescued Rottweilers

Purebred rotties that don't have AKC registration papers may still be registered through AKC's indefinite listing privilege (ILP) registration. ILP enables dogs from rescues and shelters to compete in performance events. They must be spayed or neutered and certified as a purebred by a dog professional.

What's a Pedigree?

What a registry does (besides register purebred dogs) is keep an accurate pedigree of purebred dogs. A pedigree is a family tree. The pedigree is not necessarily a symbol of quality. It doesn't mean that your dog is better than any other dog simply because he has a pedigree. In fact, if you think about it, every dog, even the lowliest mutt, has a pedigree of sorts. Being born guarantees that you have a family tree.

What's important are the dogs in the family tree. There may be quality dogs with lots of titles in conformation and performance. Or there may not be. Your rottweiler may have champions or products of backyard breeders and puppy mills in his background. It is up to you to do the research to determine which is which.

Reading Your Rottie's Pedigree

When you look at your prospective dog's pedigree, you might see several letters before and after a dog's registered name. Some of these may be:

- Obedience titles: CD, CDX, UD, UDX, OTCH
- Agility titles: NA, OA, AX, MX, MACH
- Tracking titles: TD, TDX, VST, CT
- Herding titles: HT, PT, HS, HI, HX, HCh
- Conformation titles: CH, ROM

Naturally, dogs with titles usually demonstrate that there is quality of some kind in your rottweiler's background. It shows that your rottie comes from dogs that have proven to be better than the average pet in some way, whether it is in performance or in conformation.

The Contract

If the breeder doesn't have a contract, look elsewhere. All the promises and guarantees mean nothing unless it is spelled out in writing. If there is something in the contract you don't understand, consult with a lawyer. The contract should state the following:

- The dog or puppy's identification. Usually the puppy litter number, a name, or some other distinguishing feature, including the puppy's parents.
- The guarantee that the puppy is healthy and free from genetic diseases. The breeder usually has a reasonable time limit on the guarantee and usually offers another puppy in exchange or a refund.
- Right of first refusal (or first right of refusal). The breeder stipulates that if the owner can no longer keep the dog, at any time in the dog's life and regardless of reason, the dog be returned to the breeder.
- A guarantee that the breeder will take back the dog under any circumstance.
- That you will adequately care for the puppy. This includes adequate food, water, shelter, training, socialization, and health care.

Why should you care about what's in a contract? Besides the fact that the contract is your bill of sale, it is also the proof that you bought the dog and gives you some legal recourse in case something happens. For example, let's say that your rottweiler has hip dysplasia. The contract should state what the breeder will do if your rottweiler is proven to have hip dysplasia.

The right of first refusal or first right of refusal gives the breeder the right to take the dog back if you no longer want him. However, that alone doesn't protect you, the buyer. There has to be a clause in the contract stating that the breeder will take back the dog, *regardless of circumstance.* This puts the breeder on the hook for placing the dog if there's a problem. A reputable breeder will do this but will also screen potential puppy buyers because she doesn't want a dog to come back.

 **Alert!**

Unscrupulous breeders may not honor contracts. If this is the case, you may have legal recourse. As it is expensive, most breeders aren't willing to put up with a potential lawsuit.

What's also very important are any clauses in the contract requiring special conditions, such as co-ownership or stud rights. Unless you've agreed to these types of conditions beforehand, it is unwise that you sign a contract limiting your ownership of your dog. Likewise, avoid buying from anyone who has statements that require special diets or conditions that can't be reasonably met. These conditions often void the breeder's agreement to replace or refund a dog that has a genetic disorder.

Lastly, you should receive the AKC puppy papers (with the box checked for limited registration if your rottweiler is being sold as pet quality). If the breeder doesn't furnish your rottweiler's puppy papers, then you should find another dog. There's no reason the breeder shouldn't provide your rottweiler's AKC papers, unless your prospective rottweiler isn't registered. In this case, the breeder is charging you purebred prices for a dog that may or may not be purebred. He or she may be breeding unregistered dogs that were never supposed to be bred. If you've gotten this far with seeing OFAs, CERFs, AKC registrations, and the like, it is extremely unlikely that this would happen, but be on the lookout. 🐾

CHAPTER  4

Preparing for Your New Rottweiler

YOU'VE SELECTED YOUR ROTTIE, but wait! Are you ready to bring your new rottweiler home? Owning a dog requires some foresight and planning. Have you dog-proofed your home and yard? Do you know where your rottweiler will sleep? Do you have all the necessary supplies? And have you chosen your veterinarian? All these are very important issues to resolve before bringing your rottie home.

Dog-Proofing Your House

Before you bring home a rottweiler puppy or dog, you must be sure that your home is sufficiently dog-proofed. Dogs and puppies have an uncanny knack of finding trouble, and rottweilers are no exception. It is natural for a puppy or dog to explore things, and dogs use their mouths to pick things up and find out more about them. Therefore, it is natural for them to chew inappropriate items, whether it is a shoe, laundry on the floor, or an electrical cord.

When you go through a room, get down on your hands and knees for a dog's-eye view. Are there tempting things within reach? Do you spot any knickknacks that an enthusiastic rottie could knock over? What about that enticing trash can or the roast on the counter? The trick is to find anything that is sharp, poisonous, chewable, or otherwise dangerous that your rottie can get into.

String, rubber bands, paper clips, and coins can be chewed and swallowed, causing an intestinal obstruction.

 **Essential**

There are now special devices that sense whether the electrical cord you have plugged into the wall has been chewed. If so, the device will shut off the flow of current once it senses it. These devices may give an added peace of mind.

Living Room and Family Room

The living room and family room may present hazards for your dog. Look around to see if there is anything an exuberant rottweiler can sweep off coffee tables with his tail or anything small he can pick up and chew. This includes, but is not limited to, glass knick-knacks, books, papers, remote controls, pieces to board games, puzzle pieces, craft kits and pieces, knitting needles, sewing needles, thread and yarn, loose change, indoor houseplants, cords to your Playstation or computer, and cords to lamps and draperies.

If you have a home office, keep the paper shredder away from the dog's reach. Computer cords can be chewed and cause electrocution. Pens can be chewed and swallowed. Paper clips, rubber bands, and string can all be dangerous. If your dog eats a penny, he could suffer from "penny poisoning" and will have to have surgery to remove it.

 **Fact**

Pennies made after 1982 are made of zinc with a thin coat of copper. They can make your rottweiler very sick indeed. Signs of penny poisoning include anemia, vomiting, lack of appetite, loss of weight, depression, and renal failure.

▲ Curious rottweiler puppies love to explore.

Bedrooms

The bedroom may carry enticing things that your rottie may get into. Clothing can present a choking or blockage hazard if your rottie chews them. Jewelry, toys, books, stuffed animals, makeup, and other things in the bedroom can be chewed up. Electric and drapery cords can present a hazard.

Kitchen and Bathroom

Kitchens can present a special hazard. Trash in the kitchen can be quite enticing. The stove can be dangerous especially if your dog is curious. Knives and other sharp implements can fall off counters and cut a dog, as can glass. Various cleaning solutions are toxic. There is hazardous food in your kitchen, too. Alcohol, raisins, grapes, chocolate, and onions are all poisonous to dogs.

In the bathroom you'll find all kinds of potential pet hazards, including medicines, vitamins, bathroom trash, dental floss, bathroom cleaners, makeup, air fresheners, potpourri, and cords to curling irons and hair dryers. Toothpaste and mouthwash are toxic to dogs, so be certain to keep them out of your rottie's reach. Shampoos, conditioners, and scented soaps may entice your dog to sample them, so keep them out of reach or keep the bathroom door closed.

 **Alert!**

Grapes and raisins may cause renal failure in some dogs. Currently we don't know what is in these foods that causes the problem, but there is enough evidence to keep them away from your rottie.

Basement and Attic

The basement and attic are often places where people store things. Boxes and large objects can accidentally fall and injure your dog if he is allowed in there. Craft items and other interesting things can be chewed and swallowed, causing a perforation or an obstruction. Look for paint, varnishes, rat and mouse poison, garden chemicals, and anything else that might be toxic, and keep them out of reach. Tools such as screwdrivers, saws, and bits and hardware such as screws, nails, nuts, and bolts need to be kept out of reach. Mousetraps, too, can present a problem, as can ant and roach traps or bait.

Once you have gone through the basement and attic, look for inherent dangers. Is there exposed insulation a dog could pull out and chew? Are the lines to your furnace and water heater exposed? If they are, a dog could chew on them, causing injury or even death. It is safer to keep your dog out the basement and attic altogether.

Garage

The garage is like the attic and basement in many ways. People use their garages for storing things that are poisonous to dogs, including windshield washer fluid and other fluids for their cars. Garden and lawn chemicals, usually stored in the garage, are also dangerous. Look for mouse and rat poisons, ant and roach bait, sharp tools, and hardware such as nails, screws, nuts, and bolts.

 **fact**

Garages are full of interesting smells, and it's likely that your curious rottweiler will want to explore all of them. Antifreeze is especially lethal to dogs and attracts them because it tastes sweet and salty. There are types of antifreeze that are less toxic than standard antifreeze. These are still toxic, though, and some have a bitter flavor added to it for added safety.

Once you have cleared the major hazards, start looking for hidden dangers under your car. Leaks and drips from your car contain poisonous chemicals that can kill with just a few teaspoons. Get any leaks fixed and wash down your garage floor until it is clean. It is best to keep your rottweiler out of the garage to avoid any potential problems.

The Yard

The yard can have hazards, too. Look for mushrooms. Many are benign, but it is best to treat them all as poisonous. Also keep an eye out for the poisonous pods from the black locust tree. (The honey locust is harmless, but even botanists have a difficult time telling the difference.) There are many poisonous shrubs—too many to list. Contact your local poison control center or state agricultural office for a list of poisonous plants in your area.

Look around for sharp edging that can cut your dog's pads, holes in the fence where he can escape, and other potential hazards. One hazard many people overlook is a pool. If you have a backyard pool, you will have to keep it cordoned off until you can teach your rottie how to climb out of the water safely. A kennel run might be just the thing to keep your rottie out of hazards and also to keep your lawn and garden looking good.

▲ If you have room for your rottweiler to roam around your yard, it's a good idea to designate a fenced-in area for him.

Choosing a Safe Area

When getting a new dog or puppy, many people establish a place for their new pet to stay in. This area is dog-proofed and usually has linoleum instead of carpet. That way, if the new dog or puppy has an accident or proves to be destructive, the damage is limited to one or two rooms.

Possible safe areas might include the kitchen, a recreation room or den, or some other place where you can quickly clean up messes. Choose a place that you can watch while you're doing things in the house. That way, if there's a problem, you can catch it quickly.

An alternative to baby gates (in case your home has an open floorplan) is to purchase exercise pens (x-pens) and create a small safe area for your dog to be in. Be forewarned that it is possible for a dog or puppy to climb out of an exercise pen. Also remember that no dog should be left in an exercise pen or your safe place unattended for very long. Exercise pens usually work if the puppy is small enough or if your rottweiler has been taught to respect barriers. The problem is that puppies quickly outgrow exercise pens and can become quite adept at climbing over them.

 **Essential**

You can establish a "safe place" by cordoning off rooms with baby gates. Do your best to purchase sturdy gates that are tall enough to keep your rottie from jumping over or barreling through them. (Though keep in mind that a fully grown rottie can push through nearly any gate, and many puppies can climb).

Your Rottie's Crate

This brings us to the subject of crates. Some people have a bad image of a crate as being a cage. Dogs, however, have another view. Dogs, like wolves, have a natural den instinct. They feel safer in an enclosed area. When you teach your dog to use a crate, you're taking advantage of that den instinct to give your dog a safe place to stay.

Although a crate is an excellent tool, there is such a thing as too much time in the crate. Never leave a rottweiler puppy younger than six months in a crate for longer than four hours, and never leave an adult longer than nine hours in a crate. If you must do so, consider hiring a pet sitter to come by and walk your rottie during the day.

Most dogs sleep in their crates once trained to go there. If you feed and give your rottie treats in his crate, he'll look at it as a safe haven and not a cage. To train your rottie to accept his crate, feed him in the crate; give him treats and toys in the crate. Use a special word to designate that you want your rottie in his crate: "bed," "crate," or "place" are all acceptable words. Put your rottweiler in his crate when you're unable to watch him. This is especially important in housebreaking your rottie.

Where Will Your Rottie Sleep?

The only place for your rottie to sleep is in his crate or own bed in your bedroom. There are several reasons for this, but the most important is bonding. A dog that sleeps in his owner's bedroom will more likely bond more closely than a dog that is demoted to the family room, or worse, the basement.

 **Essential**

It is good for your rottie to sleep in your bedroom, but not in your bed. If your rottweiler has dominance issues, you don't want to encourage him to look at you as an equal or litter-mate. You want to be his friend and companion, but you need to have him look on you as an owner.

Dogs who are left in the basement or other out-of-the-way place are often sent outside and soon out the door entirely. The owners are more likely to get rid of a dog they leave in a basement to sleep. Out of sight . . . out of mind . . . out the door. There's no bonding between owner and dog, and the dog is left to his own devices. As the dog's behavior worsens, the owner's attachment fades quickly. If you are unwilling to have your rottie sleep inside next to your bed, perhaps you shouldn't consider owning a dog.

Inside or Outside Dog?

Rottweilers need to be with their owners. This means that he should be with you, not stuck in the backyard. But what about the times you are gone (at work, school, or on a shopping errand)? Can't you leave your rottie out, during the day or at night?

The short answer is no. Leaving your dog unattended in the backyard isn't a good idea. At night, your rottweiler would be unattended and might bark to gain your attention. This could be a nuisance to your neighbors who are trying to sleep. During the day, people who see your dog might think it's a good idea to approach him and could end up harming him or harassing him for lack of common sense. A fenced-in yard doesn't mean that people will stay away from a dog. It's possible that service people, such as lawn care maintenance workers, electric meter readers, and postal carriers, would feel threatened by a big dog like a rottweiler. Without supervision, there are many troublesome situations that your rottweiler could get into. If you can't supervise him outside, it's best to keep your dog indoors.

Necessary Dog Supplies

Before you bring your rottie home, you'll need to purchase dog supplies. There's nothing worse than having to run around town to get the supplies you need only to have to buy them at a premium price. The following are necessary if you own a rottie:

- Dog food and water bowls
- Crate, either wire or the plastic "travel" kind
- Flat or buckle collar for everyday use (a must-have for identification tags)
- Identification tags
- Training collar (for training only, not for everyday use)
- Premium dog food or puppy food
- Bedding material
- Six-foot leather leash
- Appropriate fencing (6-foot minimum height) or kennel run
- Dog toenail clippers
- Styptic powder, in case you cut the quick in a dog's toenail
- Slicker brush or Zoom Groom for short coats
- Enzymatic cleaner for accidents

- Dog toothbrush and toothpaste—use only toothpaste made for dogs
- Dog shampoo
- Training treats
- Toys and chews

 **Essential**

Choose a leather leash instead of a nylon leash. While a little more expensive, leather will save your hands and give you more control than a nylon or cotton leash would.

If you have time, you can find most of these items on the Internet or through pet-supply catalogs for less than what you would pay in stores. Be careful though! Although you may save on the cost of the item, the shipping may be more expensive than if you had purchased the item locally. If you're in a hurry, you can purchase these items at a local pet-supply discount store.

Purchasing your dog supplies ahead of time will prevent the hassle of running around town, trying to buy the right thing for your rottweiler. You may be able to save some money, too.

Not-So-Necessary Dog Supplies

The following is a short list of supplies that aren't necessary for owning a rottweiler, but they sure make your life easier.

- **Dog grooming table**—Saves your back while you groom your rottie.
- **Flea comb**—Helps rid your rottie of fleas.
- **Pooper scoopers**—Better than a shovel.
- **Poop bags**—Specially made bags make cleaning up after your dog easier.

- **Nail grinders**—An alternative to nail clippers; some dogs tolerate it better.
- **Blow dryer for dogs**—Will help dry your dog quickly (human hair dryers should not be used, as they're too hot).
- **X-pen**—Useful as a replacement or addition to a crate.
- **Puppy/baby gates**—Be certain to buy a sturdy gate.
- **Car harness**—For those trips in the car.

While the list seems maybe a little extravagant, most items are designed to make your life easier.

Choosing a Veterinarian

Choosing the right vet is important for your rottie's health. Not all vets will be right for you and your rottie—this is one area where one size doesn't fit all. There are general practitioners, specialists, and veterinarians that specialize in certain animals or breeds. You can contact the American Veterinary Medical Association for a list of veterinarians in your area. Their Web site is ✍*www.avma.org* (for phone number and address, see Appendix A).

Where's the Vet?

You'll need some time to do your homework before you bring your dog home. Talk first with your dog-owning friends. Most will recommend a local veterinarian they like. If the breeder lives in your area, ask him whom he would recommend. If your breeder is out of state, he still may be able to ask other breeders in your area whom they use. Other resources for finding a vet can include dog trainers or groomers. You can also look for veterinarians in the Yellow Pages, your state's veterinary association, or the American Veterinary Medical Association (AVMA).

Ask the Vet

Call the potential veterinarians. Many clinics offer services besides veterinary services, such as grooming and boarding for their clients. This may be important if you need to board your rottweiler or you don't have time to groom him. Ask the following questions to determine if the veterinarian is right for you:

- Does the clinic handle emergencies, or is there an after-hours number where you can reach the veterinarian or an on-call veterinarian?
- Does the clinic offer boarding?
- Does the veterinarian have his own lab equipment, or does he need to send out for tests?
- Does the veterinarian make house calls or have a mobile clinic?
- Does the veterinarian offer a discount on certain services for multiple pets?
- Has the veterinarian worked with rottweilers before? How many?
- How many veterinarians are in the practice?
- Is there a groomer available?
- Is a trainer associated with the clinic?
- Does the clinic offer any other special services? What kind?
- Is this a clinic or hospital?
- Is your veterinarian a specialist? What is his specialty?
- When is the clinic open? What are their normal operating hours?
- Does the clinic allow walk-ins and walk-in emergencies?
- What is the cost for routine visits? Vaccinations? Dewormings? Spays and neuters?

Visit the Vet

Once you narrow the list of potential veterinarians, ask to visit the veterinarian. Don't drop by unannounced—as in any business, some days in the vet clinic are busier than others. When you visit, look around. Is the staff pleasant and friendly? Is the clinic clean and orderly? If there has been an emergency or if this is a particularly busy day, the clinic might be messy, but the overall appearance should leave a good impression.

Alert!

> Your vet should have on-call staff or a pager so you can avoid having to take your rottweiler to an emergency clinic. Otherwise, you may be paying quite a bit to have a vet who doesn't know your rottie try to make a diagnosis.

Vet Clinics

There are several types of clinics available. Some may be a general clinic, similar to a general practitioner's office, with anywhere from one to five veterinarians working there. Mobile clinics make house calls and may be associated with a general clinic or hospital. They're convenient, but may not have all the facilities necessary to make a diagnosis or to treat a dog. Hospitals are well staffed with veterinarians and usually have specialists and lab equipment. Emergency clinics are what the name implies—they handle twenty-four-hour emergencies but can be expensive. Lastly, there are low-cost clinics that perform routine care such as vaccinations, heartworm testing, dewormings, and other services, but that are only set up to handle routine care.

Pet Health Insurance

No doubt, you're looking at the cost of veterinary care and wondering why it is so expensive. However, when compared to medical care, veterinary care is actually very inexpensive. Vets must pay for the same things that human doctors do: equipment, supplies, medication, bandages, staff, and payment on the practice. And they also have to pay the mortgage and feed their families occasionally. But that knowledge still doesn't help you if you're faced with a large vet bill.

Pet health insurance is an alternative to paying for your rottie's health bills. Different plans are available, but most cover major catastrophies such as injuries and illnesses. Some offer preventive care for a higher fee.

Before you rush out and purchase pet health insurance, be aware that insurance companies come and go. Some pet owners have been left with big bills and no coverage. If you do purchase pet health insurance, buy from a company that has a high rating from A.M. Best. Also, many insurance companies don't cover hereditary or other pre-existing conditions. Many require copayments or may have deductibles. Most have caps for the amount they're willing to pay out for certain illnesses, such as cancer.

 **Essential**

A.M. Best rating is the rating for insurance companies and those who underwrite them. They're given letter grades such as A, A+, B, B-, A++, etc. The higher the rating, the more financially stable the insurance company is.

Still, having insurance might be the difference between curing your rottie or having him put to sleep, especially if you're ever faced with a serious illness. Having peace of mind might be enough to consider a pet health insurance plan.

The AKC offers health insurance to new purebred pet owners for six months. Adoption agencies such as Petfinder.com offers free health insurance for two months. There are a variety of health insurance plans listed in Appendix A. (Please note that this is not an endorsement of any plan, and that this information is included for educational purposes only.)

CHAPTER 5

Bringing Your Rottie Home

I

T IS VERY EXCITING TO bring home your new rottweiler, but what do you do when you first bring him home? When is the best time to bring your rottie home, and when are the less-than-ideal times? If you've purchased your rottweiler from a breeder, you need to know what you should receive from that breeder, and what to do once you have a rottweiler in your car. In this chapter, you'll learn how to make the transition smooth, what to expect and what not to expect, and how your rottie will react to new sights and sounds.

Planning Ahead

You're going to bring home your new rottweiler! Congratulations! But have you planned to take some time off to spend with your new family addition? If you can't take some time off, consider getting your rottie on a Friday before a three-day weekend or at least on a Friday so you have the weekend to spend with him.

The next several days are going to be very intense. If you've gotten a new puppy (or sometimes even an adult dog), you're apt not to get much sleep, and you'll wonder at some point what possessed you to get a dog, much less a rottweiler.

Be patient. This too shall pass! You can't reasonably expect for the new addition to your household to know the rules. Rottweiler puppies have a lot of energy, and a new situation will send them into hyperdrive! Play with the puppy until he tires out, then slip him into his crate and get some sleep. You'll need it, because the puppy will awake and ready to go again.

 **Essential**

If you have other family members in your household, give each of them tasks to make your rottweiler feel more at home. This can include feeding your rottie, taking him for a walk, playing with him, or making sure he always has clean, fresh water.

If you've adopted an adult or adolescent rottweiler, you too may expect a certain rowdiness that comes from being in a new experience. Exercise is the key with rottweilers. Take your rottie for a nice long walk, or play fetch with him before you have to put him in his crate. A tired rottweiler is a happy rottweiler.

▲ Taking walks in the woods is a great way for rottweilers to get exercise.

One of the ways you can ensure a smooth transition is to establish a schedule immediately. Take your rottie for a walk first thing in the morning. If you do it twice, he'll be expecting it on the third day. Dogs love a routine—it gives them something to look forward to. Schedule feeding times and nap times (after play times or exercise, naturally). Schedule times to go out (see Chapter 6). This will ensure your rottweiler will fit in smoothly into your household.

When Not to Bring a New Dog Home

Is there any time when you shouldn't bring your new dog home? In two words: the holidays. Why? you might ask. After all, it seems like a long period of vacation time when you might have time to spend with your new addition. But is it really time off?

The holidays (Christmas, Hanukkah, Kwanzaa, and so on) are usually times for you to get together with family and friends. Unless you live alone and have no parties to attend, family to see, or festive decorations to put up, you won't have time to spend with your new rottweiler. In fact, many responsible breeders won't sell a puppy for the holidays because so many puppies are given away as presents.

There are also plenty of poisonous temptations around the holiday time. Liquor, chocolate, raisins, and other goodies in great supply around the holidays are poisonous to your rottweiler. Mistletoe is extremely poisonous, and plants such as holly and poinsettias can at least cause irritation or gastric upsets. Glass ornaments can break and cut your rottie's mouth or feet, and tinsel can cause a blockage if your rottie eats it. Unless you're planning on not celebrating the holidays, choose another time to bring your rottweiler home.

Bringing Your Rottie Home

Bringing your rottweiler home takes a little preparation. Most people like to bring a second person along to help, but this is unnecessary.

You will need to bring a crate of the appropriate size to put your rottweiler in when you pick him up.

Don't rely on a family member or yourself to carry your rottweiler while you bring him home. Don't put your rottweiler in a cardboard box and expect him to stay put! Or worse, don't allow him free roam of your car, and never put a dog in the back of an open pickup bed. All of these are recipes for disaster.

 Essential

Be certain to exercise your rottweiler and give him a chance to relieve himself before putting him in the crate. If he is tired, it is likely he will settle down and sleep while on the way home.

A wiggling puppy can squirm out of your arms and become a distraction to the driver. What's worse is that you don't know how your rottie will respond to the car. He may urinate, defecate, or throw up. (Even adult dogs may do this.) If your puppy tries to do this in his crate, at least it is contained, and the worst that will happen is that he will need a cleaning when he leaves the car. Think "dog" first. Give your rottweiler ample chance to relieve himself before putting him in the car.

Items in Your Take-Home Package

Depending on whether you get your rottweiler from a breeder, shelter, or rescue, you should receive a take home-package. This package should include:

- AKC registration and pedigrees (from the breeder; may be available at the shelter or rescue)
- Contract (from all)
- Copy of health certificates (from all)
- New puppy or dog package (from all)

The breeder should provide you with all the above items. Shelters and rescue groups may only provide a limited amount of information depending on the dog's particular circumstance.

AKC Registration and Pedigrees

The breeder should provide a package with the AKC registration and pedigrees. Many breeders like to put this all in a folder so you can refer to them at any time. A shelter or rescue may provide you with AKC registration and pedigrees, but it is unlikely that they will have those if the dog didn't come from a reliable source.

If the breeder refuses to give you AKC papers because the puppy or dog is pet quality, do not buy from that breeder. As stated earlier, the breeder has the ability to limit breeding and conformation through the limited registration.

 **Alert!**

Don't forget to ask for the final contracts. Look them over to be sure that there is nothing new in them before signing them. The breeder should provide you with your own copy.

Some breeders may want to co-own a dog with you. Unless you understand the full ramifications of co-ownership, never agree to co-own a dog with anyone. Co-ownership can be a very negative experience and require you to do things you might not want to do, such as keep your rottie intact, breed your rottie, or require that you relinquish your rottie for part of the year. Serious legal battles have ensued over co-ownership rights.

Health Certificates

The breeder should provide copies of the OFA, PennHIP, and CERF certificates, as well as von Willebrand's tests. The breeder should also provide a medical record and a list of vaccinations and dewormings. While it is unlikely that shelters and rescue would have OFA, PennHIP, and CERF certificates, they should provide at least a medical record of what was done to the dog when they received him (vaccinations, dewormings, and treatments).

Puppy and Dog Packages

Breeders will normally provide a package of materials for their puppy buyers to read. These are often articles on how to housebreak, train, feed, and care for your rottweiler. They will often include a few packets of the dog or puppy food they were feeding. Some breeders may include coupons for puppy food and may even give a toy with each puppy. Shelters and rescues may also give some form of a puppy or dog kit.

Trip to the Veterinarian

Once you get your rottweiler, you should take him to the vet for a full checkup. Most reputable breeders and even shelters and breed rescues require that you have your rottweiler inspected within twenty-four to seventy-two hours. This ensures that the puppy or dog wasn't sick before leaving the breeder or shelter. It also ensures that your rottweiler will get vaccinated appropriately.

Your vet should discuss health care as well as your responsibility as a pet owner. He or she may recommend vaccinations or deworming. The vet may also discuss nutrition, training, grooming, and general care. He may recommend spaying or neutering, depending on if your rottweiler is a pet.

 Essential

Before you take your rottweiler to the vet, call up the vet's office and find out if they would like you to bring his vaccination records, health records, and maybe a fecal sample (in a plastic bag). Many veterinary clinics like to have as much information as they can get on their new client.

While it's rare, puppies can and do have reactions to vaccinations. After each vaccination, watch your rottweiler for signs of an allergic reaction: swelling of the face and neck, swelling at the injection site, hives, or difficulty breathing. In all these cases, you should seek veterinary attention immediately.

Ask any and all questions you have about your rottweiler's health. Most vets have heard these questions before, and no question is stupid. Your vet can also advise you on all aspects of pet ownership. Veterinarians are a resource—use them!

Your Trip Home

If all goes well at the veterinarian's, your next stop is home. But before you have a giant puppy party, remember that things are a little overwhelming right now for your rottweiler. Plan on having a sedate entrance. When you take your rottie out of the car, put him on a leash and let him sniff around outside. He will most likely need to relieve himself, but in all the excitement, he may forget to do so. Be patient. Let him sniff, and once he has relieved himself, go ahead and take him inside.

 Essential

Introduce each of the family members one at a time so you don't overwhelm the new addition to your family. They can pet him, but don't let them smother him with affection. Make sure they give him enough room to explore and come to them.

When you bring your rottweiler home, don't throw too many things at him or he'll be overwhelmed. Don't have a puppy party. The situation will be exciting or frightening enough without having hoards of people intimidating your dog. Keep everything low key. Your rottie needs some time to assimilate everything. He may be hyper, or he may decide it is time for a nap. Introduce him slowly to his new home. Try putting him first in the safe area and letting him sniff around.

▲ Introducing your rottweiler puppy to different situations and experiences will help him become comfortable with his surroundings.

Meeting Other Pets

Introductions to your new rottweiler are best left for another time. Keep your other pets in a different room while your rottie is allowed to explore the safe area. Once he is secure and comfortable in his new environment, you can then begin to introduce other pets slowly.

Introducing the Other Dog

If you own another dog, you'll want to introduce your rottie in a neutral area, preferably a park outside your home. You will need another person to take your other dog on a leash to the park. Walk your rottie to the park and have them meet. Since both are aware of the other dog in the house, this gives them the opportunity to finally meet. Keep a loose leash—a tight leash often telegraphs nervousness. Watch for signs of aggression, like stiff-legged gait, hackles up, growling, or snarling. Correct any aggression. You may have to have several encounters before they can finally play together.

Introducing the Cat

Introducing the cat is a little different. Keep the cat in another part of the house so your rottie can become aware of her and her scent. This way, when you do have them meet each other, it will not be a complete surprise. When you're ready to introduce the two, pick a room where your cat can climb out of your rottweiler's reach. Calmly bring your rottie into the room on a leash and bring treats with you. Correct any aggressive behavior or desire to chase the cat, and reward him anytime he pays attention to you and not the cat.

 **Essential**

Your cat will need a place to escape the unwanted attentions of your rottie. Have climbing trees, bookshelves, and window shelves available that your cat can use to escape. You may have to show your cat these perches by feeding her tuna or other tasty treats on them.

Some rotties do really well with cats, especially if raised with them. The more you can encourage your rottweiler to ignore the cat, the better the chances are that your rottie and your cat will get along. Some cats actually get downright bossy toward dogs and will swat a curious puppy that sticks his nose where it shouldn't be. If you have an adult rottie that is used to cats, your rottie probably will show some interest in the cat but will eventually ignore her. The trick to keeping your cat safe is to provide a place for her to go if the rottweiler chases her.

The First Few Days and Nights

The first few days and nights with your new rottweiler may be trying. Your rottie may cry at night because he is in strange surroundings. Gone are his littermates and his mom, whom he depended on. Now, he must depend on you.

Imagine being alone in a strange place without anything familiar. At night, it is quiet and spooky. Unless your puppy is tired, he's had a chance to realize he's all alone in a strange place. No wonder he cries!

Ensuring a Good Night's Sleep

To give your rottweiler the security he needs at night, put his crate at your bedside. He'll be able to see you, and your presence will comfort him. If he cries, you'll be able to tap his crate and tell him to be quiet.

Even though your puppy is small, he still has a lot of energy and will want to play when he's not tired. Exercising your dog before putting him to bed (although not necessarily right before putting him to bed) will help him use some of his energy, and he'll settle down more easily.

▲ A well-exercised rottweiler makes for a tired dog at the end of the day.

When you put your dog to sleep, make sure you take him outside first so that he has the chance to relieve himself. This will help him sleep more comfortably and possibly for a longer time. If he does wake up and begin to whimper, it could be a sign that he needs to go outside again. Limiting food and water an hour or so before your rottweiler goes to bed might reduce his need to go, but if it is hot or he is thirsty and has exercised, you should never withhold water. Your puppy will learn to control his bladder as he becomes housetrained, so midnight runs to your backyard will eventually decrease and stop all together.

 Fact

The daytimes will be a bit trying, too, until your rottie learns the routine. Always let him outside to relieve himself after he wakes up, after he eats or drinks, and after he exercises. See Chapter 6 for more information on housetraining.

Rottweiler adults are far less likely to cry than puppies, but you should still have your rottweiler tired out and in a crate next to your bed. Your presence will certainly comfort him—after all, if he's been in a shelter, this is probably a lot less stressful and much more comforting.

The Alarm Clock and the Hot Water Bottle

Some pet experts suggest using a hot water bottle wrapped in a towel placed in the crate to simulate the heat of a rottie's littermates. Putting an old-fashion ticking clock on top of the crate (without the alarm set) is supposed to mimic the heartbeat of mom. It is arguable whether or not this works, but it is worth a try.

Ownership Responsibilities

You'll lose sleep the first several nights—this is why it is recommended to have some time off. There's nothing that shortens the pet owner's patience more than lack of sleep. If you're only running on a few hours a night, you'll be wondering what convinced you to get a pet. Sleep deprivation does strange things, so be sure to make some nap time for yourself over the next few days.

Above all, have patience. Exercise your rottie briskly until he's tired, let him relieve himself, and put him in his bed. Guaranteed, if he's tired, he'll fall right to sleep. And so will you.

▲ Playtime is a great way for young rottweilers to get exercise and become oriented with the world around them.

CHAPTER 6

Housetraining

I F THERE IS ONE KIND OF TRAINING you have to do right with your rottie, it is housetraining (or housebreaking, as it is often called). Most owners can put up with a dog that won't quite sit on command or won't come when called, but a dog that uses the house as a toilet won't be tolerated long. Indeed, many dogs end up in the shelter or in rescues because their original owners failed to housetrain them properly. It is the biggest problem most owners face. Luckily, rottweilers aren't one of the more difficult breeds to housebreak. Rottweilers are naturally intelligent and are usually capable of figuring out what their owners want of them. Occasionally, you'll run into a stubborn rottie, but you should be able to housetrain your rottie relatively easily.

Crates and Housetraining

So, how do you housetrain a rottweiler? The first step in housetraining is to buy a crate and teach your rottie to use it. Unfortunately, crates are the most misunderstood tool in the dog trainer's arsenal.

How Dogs See a Crate

When non-dog people look at crates, they see a cage or perhaps a box or shipping container. They think, "Oh, how cruel! I would never want to be in a crate!" However, these people are anthropomorphizing. (That is, ascribing human feelings and emotions to something that isn't human—in this case, a dog.) A dog sees the crate as a safe place—a hidey-hole away from something potentially dangerous—or a place to sleep undisturbed. If you've ever seen a dog that becomes fearful during an electrical storm, you'll see him look for something to hide under. It is a natural instinct that dogs inherited from their wolf ancestors. Wolves make their homes in dens, a hole with low ceilings. Wolves won't defecate or urinate in their den, unless they're sick or have no choice. You can harness that natural desire to maintain cleanliness in your rottweiler.

Types of Crates

There are two types of crates you should consider when purchasing one for your rottweiler: wire and travel crates. There are some cloth and PVC crates out there, but these are intended for obedience-trained dogs, not as a regular crate.

Wire crates allow for more air circulation and many are now foldable, so you can transport them anywhere. Choose a crate with a good latch and a heavy wire gauge to discourage Houdini-type antics. If you choose a wire crate, be certain that the metal is thick enough so your rottweiler can't chew it or bend it with a push of his nose.

 **Alert!**

There is such a thing as too much time in the crate. If you don't have enough time to spend with your rottie or if you're stuck in a job that requires long hours some days, consider hiring a pet sitter to exercise your dog.

Travel crates are plastic and more enclosed. They usually offer the dog a bit more protection than wire crates. Purchase one that is airline approved. If you can, choose one with circular fasteners that lock the crate together with one twist (the bolt and wing-nut fasteners are time-consuming and aggravating). Also, be certain that the latching is sturdy and secure. A bonus to travel crates is that if they're airline approved, you can use your dog's crate to hold him if you're traveling someplace.

▲ Crates are convenient for traveling with your rottweiler and training him, too.

Fitting the Crate

The crate should be big enough so an adult rottweiler can stand up, turn around, and lie down. While this seems a little cramped, remember that wolves don't have a lot of room in their dens. Their dens insulate them against the cold air. If you buy an adult crate for your rottie puppy, be sure to cordon off the crate so that he won't make a mess in one portion and lie down in another. Some puppy owners buy a smaller puppy crate (usually inexpensive) and switch to the adult crate when their rottie grows out of the first one.

When to Use a Crate

Keep your rottweiler in his crate when you can't watch him inside. This prevents your rottweiler from sneaking off and relieving himself in the next room or chewing something he's not supposed to. Give him a toy or a nice chew to keep him occupied. Feed him in his crate and give him treats in there, too. Let him know that this is his safe place.

 **Fact**

Almost all dogs prefer crates, but there are occasionally those that can't tolerate them. These dogs are usually adults that were never trained properly to accept a crate. In this instance, an x-pen or cordoned-off area, like a small room, might work.

Training to Accept a Crate

Most people think that they can just pop their puppy in a crate without any prior training. This is fine if you're not planning to get any sleep. Don't force your dog to go into the crate; instead, toss treats into the crate to get him to enter. After he enters the crate, give him a toy or favorite chew. If you aren't giving a good enough treat to lure him into the crate, use something really tempting, such as a piece of hot dog or some cold cuts.

Exercise your rottweiler before you put him in the crate for longer periods (bedtime, leaving for work or school). Take him for a long walk or play fetch with him. (Also make sure that he eliminates.) The idea is to tire out your rottweiler so all he wants to do is sleep. A sleepy puppy is a happy puppy and one that is not likely to fuss.

Music to Your Rottie's Ears

When you leave for a long time, you might want to consider leaving on some light music or the television, tuned to an innocuous channel such as the Weather Channel or something that has soothing music. Don't tune into talk radio or television that has a lot of noise and violence—you want your rottweiler to sleep, not become a political animal.

Being tired combined with soothing music helps calm down a puppy. The music eventually reinforces that it is naptime. Some people have actually recorded music for pets. You can try some of those CDs or try soothing sounds of nature or some light jazz.

 **Essential**

Along with CDs of various kinds of music, you can also make a tape of your voice. Read a boring book into a cassette recorder and play it while you're gone. The soothing sound of your voice might be music to your rottweiler's ears.

How Long Is Too Long?

As a word of caution, remember that a dog can be left in a crate too long. Never leave your adult rottweiler in a crate for longer than nine hours at a time. If your rottweiler is a puppy younger than six months, don't leave him in the crate longer than four hours. If you are unable to let him out at least to relieve himself, have a friend or relative come over or hire a pet sitter.

Establishing a Routine

Once your rottweiler is used to the crate, you can use it to house-train. The trick is to establish a schedule so your rottie knows when he will be able to relieve himself. While most people love surprises, dogs love a routine. It gives them something to anticipate.

You will have to let your rottweiler outside frequently to relieve himself, especially if he is a puppy. Puppies have small bladders and little control. Here's a good routine for letting out your rottweiler:

- When he first wakes up in the morning
- After he eats or drinks
- After he exercises
- Before you go to work or school

- Around lunchtime
- When you come home
- After dinner
- Before bedtime
- Any time he leaves his crate

This may sound like a lot, but if you think about it, it really isn't. You're trying to train your rottweiler to go when you put him out, not when the urge strikes. Housetrain to prevent accidents. If your rottie is conditioned to eliminate outside every time, it teaches him that outside is where he should eliminate.

 **Essential**

You can teach your dog to let you know when he has to go out. Hang a bell on the doorknob within reach of his nose. Before he goes out, make him nudge the bell and make it ring. Then let him out. If you do this consistently, your rottie will start ringing the bell every time he wants to go outside.

Watch your rottie when he's loose in the house. If he starts sniffing or circling, it is time to put him out. You can use a key command such as "Out" when you escort him outside. If you can't watch him while he is inside, put him in his crate.

The way you develop your schedule with your rottweiler is largely dependent upon your day. However, be very aware that puppies can't "hold it" for a long time. It's important to give your rottweiler plenty of chances to succeed in housebreaking. Above all, keep the schedule *consistent*.

Puppy Mill Dogs

Housebreaking the puppy mill or pet shop puppy may present quite a challenge. These dogs have learned that it is okay to go against their instinct and soil their crates. This habit is very difficult to train out, which is one of the many reasons you should never buy from a pet shop or puppy mill. But it can be done with patience.

Set a routine and use a clicker (described in Chapter 14) to encourage housebreaking. Whenever you take him outside and he eliminates, click and treat. If he eliminates in the crate, clean it up. If he leaves feces in his crate, move it outside to continue to encourage him to eliminate outside.

With a puppy mill dog, it is very important to keep him in the smallest crate possible (one that he can stand up, turn around, and lie down in), but not to leave him in there for long. Assure him that he's able to relieve himself outside at certain times of the day, and he'll count on you to do this.

What to Do about Accidents

All the vigilance and schedules won't always prevent accidents. Accidents happen, even with older dogs. When you catch your rottweiler in the act, you will most likely shriek in dismay, which will startle him. Don't scream. Don't yell. Don't rub his nose in it or hit him. Tell him "No! Out! Out!" and whisk him outside. When he finishes relieving himself outside, praise him.

 Essential

If you smell urine, but don't know where your dog has gone, you can use a black light. Urine fluoresces under black light. (Nature's Miracle has a black light for pet owners that is available at pet-supply stores.)

What happens when your rottie has an accident and you don't catch him in the act? Can you correct him? Experts disagree on this, but several people have found it is very helpful to show the mess to the dog and tell him that he's been a bad dog. Again, don't yell or scream. Don't hit or rub his nose in it. Your tone of voice should be enough to convince him you're displeased with him.

Once you've corrected your dog and put him outside where he can relieve himself, you need to clean up the mess. Don't use fancy cleaners that are ammonia-based. Most dogs can smell the urine long after those cleaners evaporate. Instead, clean the area with a good enzymatic cleaner made for pet messes, or use plain soap and water and follow it up with white vinegar diluted with water. Vinegar and water help neutralize the smell and make it less likely that your dog will seek to eliminate in that area again. If you don't thoroughly clean up the area, you run the risk that your rottweiler will pick up the traces of odor and use that area when he needs to eliminate again. You may not smell anything, but your dog will.

How Long Does It Take to Housetrain?

Despite all the promises of various books and articles, housetraining takes time and vigilance. Much of your success depends on your rottweiler's learning curve, his age, and your consistency. Some dogs are fully housetrained in a few weeks; some dogs take a whole year before they're completely reliable. Most rottweilers are somewhere in the middle. Take heart! If you stay consistent, your dog will become housetrained.

Should You Paper-Train?

In a word: no! In the past, owners often used paper-training as an intermediate step in housebreaking. The problem with paper-training is that it reinforces elimination in the house. Paper-training is quite often an unnecessary step to housebreaking.

But what if your rottie is paper-trained? Some breeders and owners have already paper-trained their puppies. If so, you'll need to teach your rottweiler not to eliminate on that piece of paper and instead to go outside.

Because a paper-trained rottweiler may interpret that newspaper (or any paper, for that matter) as a signal to relieve himself, you must keep all paper off the floor. Place a piece of newspaper outside in the area you intend your rottweiler to use. When you take him outside to eliminate, he might be confused that you want him to relieve himself outside. Be patient. He will eventually go outside. When he does, praise him. Once he starts understanding that he is to go outside on the paper, start reducing the size of the paper. Eventually, you'll be able to take the paper away completely.

 **fact**

Housetraining the older dog is actually easier than housetraining a puppy. Most adult dogs have sufficient bladder control to wait until you let them outside. Even so, put your rottweiler on the same housetraining regimen, and keep him in a crate when you can't watch him.

Relapses in Housetraining

Once your rottweiler is housetrained, you may feel the days of accidents are long behind you. However, he may have an accident in the house occasionally, especially if he is still a puppy. Consistent training is still required until your rottweiler is an adult. Relapses in housebreaking can occur for several reasons, including medical problems, insufficient training, dominance marking behavior, and submissive urination. In each situation, there's a remedy, but you must identify the problem first.

Medical Problems

If your rottie is an adult and you've fully trained him, illness may be the most likely cause for an accident (as in diarrhea). In this case, there's nothing to do except treat the diarrhea and clean up the mess. However, if your rottweiler suddenly starts urinating or defecating in the house frequently, it might be a sign of illness. Changes in your rottie's behavior, such as suddenly forgetting he's housebroken, may be a sign of a serious medical condition. Before you attempt any behavior modification, assume the problem is medical. Take him to a veterinarian for a full checkup.

 **Essential**

Tell your veterinarian what you're experiencing. Is your rottie urinating only or urinating and defecating? Is it in one spot or multiple spots? When does it occur? When you're home? When your rottweiler is greeting you?

Your vet will most likely check for bladder and kidney infections as well as other possible problems (diabetes insipidus, Cushing's disease, diabetes mellitus). Some spayed female rottweilers may show incontinence and may leak or dribble a little, and your vet has medication that can fix this. Very old rottweilers may suffer from cognitive dysfunction syndrome (CDS) and may forget that they are housebroken. This is also treatable with medication from your vet.

Behavioral Problems

If there is no apparent biological problem, your next step is to determine if your rottweiler's problem is behavioral (as with marking or submissive behaviors) or insufficient training. If your dog is insufficiently trained, he may urinate or defecate in the house, usually in large amounts. In either case, the dog may eliminate in your presence or may sneak away to go into a back room. Behavioral problems usually involve marking territory—usually with urine—on key items: beds, new items, something that belongs to a specific family member or a guest, or vertical surfaces. Submissive urination is due to the owner's behavior.

> Tethering works well in most behavioral cases of relapse in housebreaking. It's not coercive and doesn't require you to get angry or upset. It also works in dominance and bonding issues.

Marking and dominance behavior suggests that neutering or spaying your rottweiler and getting some good obedience training is in order. With insufficient training, going back to the house-training regimen is a must. In either case, tethering your rottweiler to you will keep him from sneaking off and will strengthen the bond between you and your dog.

Tethering or Umbilical Cording

Tethering or umbilical cording is a trick in the trainer's repertoire. Get a 10-foot tracking lead or rope and attach one end to your rottweiler's collar and the other end to you. Now, wherever you go, your rottweiler goes—whether it is to the kitchen, the living room, or the bathroom. Your rottie will be forced to focus on you and can't sneak off to eliminate. When the two of you can't be tethered, put him in the crate. This training method works wonders, but it takes time. Most people must tether their dogs a month or more to make a difference.

Submissive Urination

Submissive urination is due to behavior, but is owner-caused. It occurs usually during boisterous greetings or when you become angry with your rottie and raise your voice. This type of urination requires a different response as it isn't meant to show dominance nor is it a housetraining issue. Instead, it is a reaction to your dominance as an owner. Loud boisterous greetings may generate a fearful or submissive reaction from your rottie, as can raising your voice.

Why do dogs submissively urinate?
In pack behavior, lower-ranking dogs urinate submissively as a sign to show the alpha dog that they respect his authority. When you become angry, shout, or are being loud, this further intensifies your rottie's reaction to you being in charge. By submissively urinating, he is only doing what nature says he's supposed to do.

The trick to correcting submissive urination is to change *your* behavior. Make entrances and exits low key, and don't yell at your rottweiler. Instead, keep your greetings calm. Kneel down to greet him instead of looming over him. Make yourself more of a friend and less of an owner. Don't correct submissive urination, as anxiety only adds to the problem. If your rottweiler gets excited and urinates when greeting you at the door, try another type of greeting. Try bringing him outside for the greeting—then you won't care if he does urinate. Or you can keep him in his crate and do something before you let him out so that the excitement of the moment has passed. Ⓔ

Basic Nutrition

NUTRITION TENDS TO BE an overlooked subject among pet owners since so many people feed their pets a commercial diet. After all, what could be easier than opening up a bag of doggie crunchies and pouring it for your dog? But all dog food is not the same. Depending on what you're feeding your rottie, you may not be supplying him with the right nutrients. Without proper nutrition, your puppy will not grow up to be strong and healthy. If he doesn't get good nutrition as an adult, he will have a dull coat, a poor immune system, and other health problems. If he is a competition dog, that translates into poor performance. If he is a pet, that may mean bigger vet bills and a shorter lifespan.

Choosing a Dog or Puppy Food

There are many different types of dog food that contain a wide range of ingredients with varying qualities. The quality of the food affects how easily the dog will digest it. You should look for food with ingredients that provide your dog with the highest nutrition available.

Digestibility

To determine the digestibility of dog food, closely examine the ingredients. You can learn a lot about dog food from the order in which the ingredients are listed. Ideally, meat such as beef or chicken will be the first ingredient, but you might find instead that rice and corn and artificial flavors top the list. These filler ingredients are added to the food so that the flavor will appeal to dogs. You'll notice that very few dog foods list meat as their first ingredient. Premium dog foods generally cost more, but you feed significantly less because they have fewer fillers. By choosing one of these dog foods, you're boosting your dog's intake of vital nutrients that will give him energy and protein, not just giving him a tasty meal and calories.

AAFCO Guidelines

When you look for a premium dog food, look for one that is from a recognizable name and that meets or exceeds the American Association of Feed Control Officials' (AAFCO) guidelines. This organization sets the standards on what is nutritionally complete and balanced. Their seal of approval will help you choose a food that satisfies your dog's nutrition requirements. For convenience, you should choose a brand that's carried in most pet stores. Not only will it be easier for you to find in case you suddenly run out, but you're also guaranteed to find it on sale every now and then. Not all pet foods meet AAFCO guidelines, although many do.

 Alert!

Lamb-and-rice dog food was once thought to be hypoallergenic because it contained a protein source not usually included in a dog's diet. It became a regular ingredient in dog food, and many dogs developed allergies to the rice and lamb because of it.

The more digestible dog food is, the more premium it is. Dog food that is over 80 percent digestible is generally considered premium, but don't assume that a dog food is premium because it meets AAFCO standards. You must still look at the label and find out what the digestibility of the product is. Dog food manufacturers seldom print digestibility on their labels, but most have toll-free numbers you can call to ask.

The Right Food for Age and Activity Level

Choose a dog food appropriate for your rottie's age and activity level. Most premium dog foods have age-related foods such as those geared to the puppy, adult, and senior. Several also have activity-level foods like active, maintenance, light, and performance. A few even have breed-specific related food, like those for toy breeds, large breeds, and medium breeds.

If you've picked a dog food that has all these varieties, try the food that takes your rottie's age, activity level, and size (large or giant) into consideration. Once you see how he does with the food, you can then decide if he needs more protein and fat than what that food provides. Most active adult foods contain approximately 26 percent protein and 15 percent fat, and most puppy foods contain approximately 28 percent protein and 18 percent fat. These figures will vary according to breed and activity levels. If your rottie is too skinny, you may have to switch to a performance food. If your rottie is too fat, you may have to switch to a maintenance or light food.

Canned, Dry, Frozen, or Semi-Soft?

Now that you know more about the different types of dog food available, what form of it is best for your dog to eat? There's dry kibble, canned, frozen, and semi-soft. Choosing which food to buy is mostly a matter of preference, although each food type has its pros and cons. Your dog might prefer one kind to another, so don't be afraid to test them out. He might like one kind too much, though. For instance, if your dog likes canned food to the point that he eats it too fast and vomits, you might want to switch to another form.

 Alert!

Occasionally, you may want to switch dog foods. To avoid gastric distress and minimize diarrhea, make the switch gradually. Start your rottie out with 90 percent of his old food and 10 percent of the new food. Increase the new food by 10 percent each day while decreasing the old food by the same amount.

Dry Food

Pound for pound, dry food is the most economical and easiest to prepare. There are more choices in dry food than any other form. When you purchase your rottie's food, check the bag's freshness date or the manufacture date. Since most premium dog foods are no longer preserved with ethoxyquin, they can become rancid quickly if subjected to heat or long periods of shelf life. Ethoxyquin is a preservative that's been given a bad rap because of anecdotal stories of miscarriages, cancer, tumors, and other ailments. However, there hasn't been any scientific proof that ethoxyquin causes any health problems so far. As most other preservatives don't have the shelf life of ethoxyquin, it is very important to buy fresh dog food.

If your brand of food doesn't have an expiration or manufacturer's date, buy it from a store that turns over its stock regularly. Don't purchase old bags—the food may be rancid and will have lost most of its nutritional value. Purchase food no longer than six months from its manufacture date to ensure freshness. Most dog foods have a shelf life of one year or less.

As for palatability, if your rottie is a picky eater, he may turn his nose up at dry food.

Canned Food

A second option is canned food. Canned food tends to be more expensive because you pay for the processing, preservatives, and packaging. Also, dogs need to eat a larger amount of canned food in one feeding than dry food. It tends to appeal to dogs more than plain dry food, so many dog owners mix the two. Canned food is convenient because it has a long shelf life, but once opened, it must be refrigerated for freshness.

 **Essential**

Preparing a meal of canned food for your dog will take a little longer than scooping a serving of dry food, but if your dog responds better to it, it's probably worth the extra effort.

Frozen Food

Frozen food is relatively new on the scene and may not be available in all areas. It is expensive when compared to dry food because you pay for water weight and storage. You need a freezer to store it, and if the power goes out, you might lose your rottie's meals for the next week. There are no preservatives in frozen food and it is highly palatable.

Semi-Soft Food

Semi-soft food now takes two forms. The older form looks like meat patties. They're soft and chock-full of salt, sugar, and artificial coloring. Use these sparingly. The newer form tends to be available in meat rolls. These meat rolls are designed to be a palatable alternative to dry dog food. Unlike the old type of semi-soft food, this food tends to have no fillers or artificial colors or sugar. They're highly palatable but require refrigeration, especially when opened. They are more expensive than dry dog food.

The Role of Vital Nutrients in a Dog's Diet

Your rottweiler requires protein, fat, carbohydrates, vitamins, and minerals to maintain his health. Dogs need to have their nutrients carefully balanced just as humans do. The results of eating too little or too much of a certain nutrient could prove harmful. Knowing how the most important components of food affect your dog will help you choose the right dog food, snacks, vitamins, or other dietary supplements.

Protein

Protein is one of the body's essential building blocks, providing four kilocalories of energy per gram. It provides the foundation necessary for the formation of muscle, connective tissue, fur, nails, skin, blood, and organs. Protein is important for puppies, pregnant and lactating bitches, and working dogs. Older dogs require protein, too. The only time you should consider limiting your rottweiler's protein intake is if he is obese or has kidney disease.

 **Fact**

Most premium performance dog foods are 30 percent protein and 20 percent fat, providing higher calories and higher protein to help repair muscle. However, few dogs actually need this much nutrition, and many will do well on an active adult version of the dog food. If your rottie sustains injuries or starts losing weight, you will then need to switch him to the performance dog food.

Protein can come from a variety of plants and animals. Animal protein is usually more complete than plant protein, having all of the necessary amino acids a dog requires. One of the first two ingredients in your rottweiler's food should be its protein source, such as chicken, beef, lamb, or poultry by-products. By-products are an excellent source of protein and should not be summarily dismissed. The quality of the protein depends solely on the manufacturer. The definition of by-products, for example, leaves much open for interpretation. Poultry by-products from one source may be a far superior quality than poultry by-products from another manufacturer. Some sources of by-products have better quality nutrition than the actual meat source.

Years ago, veterinarians believed that high-protein diets caused kidney disease. This has no basis in fact. Research proves that working dogs actually require more protein to maintain muscle and to avoid serious injuries. If you work your rottweiler in Schutzhund, herding, or agility, you will want to feed him a high-protein performance dog food. However, if your rottweiler has kidney disease, you should consult your veterinarian for an appropriate diet. A dog excretes excessive protein through his kidneys, and if they are diseased, all this protein may overwork them.

Fat

Fat is an energy-dense nutrient with nine kilocalories per gram. Dogs use fat to maintain a healthy skin and coat, to provide insulation against heat and cold, to protect vital organs, and to absorb the fat-soluble vitamins A, D, E, and K. Unlike humans, dogs generally do not have to worry about high cholesterol, so fat becomes an excellent source of energy. Working dogs process fat in much the same way as human athletes use carbohydrates.

 Fact

Fats can be saturated (solid) or unsaturated (liquid). Unsaturated fats tend to turn rancid quickly. Animal fat sources can be from poultry, beef, pork, horse, lamb, or a mixture of these.

The latest nutrition fad has been omega-3 fatty acids. These fats come from linseed and fish oils and have some anti-inflammatory qualities. They may also decrease the size of some tumors. However, omega-3 fatty acids should not make up more than 5 percent of your dog's food in dry matter weight. Large amounts of omega-3 have been shown to inhibit blood clotting in humans.

Simple injuries could result in life-threatening hemorrhaging if you include too much omega-3 fatty acids in your rottweiler's diet. Feeding a dog food with supplemented omega-3 fatty acids is usually the safest way to give him omega-3s. However, use caution if you wish to supplement using omega-3 fatty acids or if omega-3 fatty acids are the dog food's only source of fat. Consult a veterinary nutritionist if your rottweiler has von Willebrand's disease and you wish to further supplement omega-3 fatty acids.

Carbohydrates

Carbohydrates provide four kilocalories of energy per gram. Carbohydrates provide some energy and bulk for the dog in the form of dietary fiber. If you are working your rottweiler, you will wish to focus on increasing the protein and fat, while decreasing the carbohydrates. Most commonly, the carbohydrate sources in dog food include corn and corn products, wheat, and rice. Some grains, such as cooked rice, are easier to digest than corn. Some dogs are allergic to certain grains such as corn or wheat gluten. In this case, rice, barley, or potatoes are an acceptable substitute.

 **Alert!**

Limit treats to 10 percent of your rottweiler's total diet. Treats that are shaped like human food are usually high in calories, sugar, salt, and artificial colors and flavors. Use these sparingly. Crunchy biscuits made by premium pet-food manufacturers are usually nutritionally balanced and not loaded with unnecessary ingredients.

Supplements

If you are feeding a premium dog food, there is no reason to supplement your rottweiler's diet. Your dog will obtain all the necessary nutrients from a complete and balanced food. Adding certain vitamins and minerals can seriously affect that balance and actually cause more harm than good. Never give your rottweiler supplements intended for humans without first obtaining advice from a veterinarian. Some vitamin levels that are safe for humans are toxic to dogs. If you wish to supplement, choose a balanced multivitamin formulated for dogs.

Free-Feeding

Free-feeding is when the owner leaves a bowl of food out for the dog to eat as he pleases. It is convenient since the owner doesn't have to establish a feeding time and only has to remember to keep the dog's food bowl filled. But do not do this.

Dogs that free-feed are less apt to look on their owners as dominant. Establishing a feeding time should be part of your rottweiler's training. You determine how much food and when your rottweiler eats. Put him in a sit/stay when you fix his food. After you put the food down, release him with a word such as "okay."

 **Alert!**

Table scraps are not good for your rottweiler. Most table scraps are high in fat, salt, carbohydrates, and calories that he doesn't need. Feeding table scraps may also turn him into a picky eater. If you want to give your dog a treat, save a couple of choice tidbits and give them to him after he has eaten his dinner.

If he is too fat, you can control how much your rottweiler eats. Likewise, you will immediately know if something is wrong if your rottweiler ignores his food. Dogs fed on a schedule are less likely to become picky eaters. If your rottweiler is normally a chowhound and suddenly begins to ignore or pick at his food, it is time for a trip to the veterinarian. A sick dog will normally not eat. You can use your rottweiler's eating habits as a barometer for his health.

Hypoallergenic Diets

Some dogs are allergic or intolerant to certain ingredients in dog food. The dog is most often allergic to the protein source (soy, chicken, beef, or lamb) or carbohydrate source (corn or wheat). Occasionally, the dog may be allergic to other ingredients. Food intolerances commonly manifest themselves in gastric disturbances, diarrhea, and gas. Food allergies appear as skin and coat problems as well as other medical problems. If your rottweiler is allergic to food, your veterinarian can prescribe a hypoallergenic diet with a novel protein source. There are diets based on fish, venison, veal, turkey, or kangaroo meat with rice, potatoes, or barley.

Raw Diets

A current popular fad among dog owners is raw food and home-made diets. Pet owners want the very best for their dogs, and so they decide that raw or home-cooked diets are the way to go. There are books dedicated to raw diets, and many Web sites, chat rooms, and e-mail lists out there espouse the virtues of raw and homemade diets.

You may indeed be tempted to try these diets because of all the hype. People offer anecdotal evidence that these diets are better than anything available commercially. However, some popular praise of such diets is based on the following questionable reasoning:

Elimination of allergies. If the dog had allergies, there was something in the previous diet that the dog was allergic to or intolerant of. The owner might cause the same allergies if he or she accidentally feeds the ingredient to the dog. It is best to have a vet diagnose what causes the allergy.

Improved appearance. How does the dog look better? Was she sick before? This is highly subjective.

Increased lifespan. There are no statistics on whether dogs fed raw diets live longer than those fed commercial dog food. Good nutrition and exercise will help a dog live longer, not just a fad diet.

Raw bones are safe for dogs to eat. Any vet who has removed blockages or repaired a dog's intestines after the dog ate a bone will tell you that raw bones can be harmful.

Wolves eat raw diets. Wolves are wild animals that hunt on instinct. Dogs are a domestic species that have been trained to eat manufactured food, not fresh kill. Raw diets don't reflect what a wild wolf would eat, anyway. A chicken leg and some fresh vegetables is not the same as a moose carcass.

Less frequent visits to the vet. Any dog with a complete and balanced diet will be healthier. If your dog is getting an imbalanced diet, he may have health problems.

There's nothing wrong with feeding your dog a raw diet, provided that you have your dog's diet analyzed and evaluated by a veterinary nutritionist. Many of these diets lack crucial vitamins and minerals, and few people who follow these diets ever have them analyzed. There have been some preliminary testing of these diets by veterinary nutritionists who have published their findings in the *Journal of the American Veterinary Medical Association.* These findings show that most of these diets have dangerous imbalances in key nutrients and many carry harmful bacteria. While your rottie may or may not have a resistance to the bacteria, you can contract those bacteria from your dog, which will make you very sick.

 **Alert!**

At first, mixing your rottweiler's own diet might seem like a good idea. However, without extensive knowledge of canine nutrition, you are likely to cause imbalances in his diet. Calcium, for example, must be balanced with phosphorus. Too much calcium can be as serious as too little. Too much iron can inhibit the absorption of other vital nutrients, while too little can cause anemia.

Premium dog food is the culmination of intensive research by dog-food manufacturers. Many of these manufacturers continue testing to provide optimal nutrition. These premium pet-food manufacturers try to exceed the guidelines set forth by the AAFCO committee. Homemade diets can seldom compare to this superior nutrition.

If you would like to try a raw food diet, many veterinarians recommend that you feed a good premium commercial dog food and add raw vegetables. It's a great idea to consult a nutritionist at a veterinary college. Most are willing to work with you to help you develop a complete and balanced diet with the ingredients available to you.

Vegetarian Diets

While dogs can and do live on vegetarian diets, you should consider what a dog or wolf would eat in the wild. Their preferred diet would certainly not be soybeans and tofu! Dogs are carnivores, and their systems process meat most efficiently. Vegetarian diets largely contain soy to boost the protein content. Some dogs are allergic to soy, which can cause gastric upset. Most vegetarian dog foods are also low in protein and fat. If you work your rottie, you may have a difficult time finding a vegetarian diet with protein high enough for his needs. In this case, you may have to switch to a meat-based diet anyway. If your rottie is allergic to meat, consult your veterinarian.

How and When to Feed

Follow the dog-food manufacturer's recommended guidelines for amount of food to feed. These portions are usually too large, but they provide a good basis. If your rottweiler is under six months of age, split the portion into three meals a day. Rottweilers six months and older should have two meals. Do not feed your rottweiler one big meal—this may lead to bloat, a life-threatening illness. Likewise, if your rottweiler gulps food or eats too rapidly, try mixing his food with water or feeding multiple smaller portions. Don't feed and leave. You will need to watch your rottweiler for the next hour for signs of discomfort.

 **Essential**

> If your rottweiler does not eat immediately, pick up the food after ten minutes. Offer it again at his next feeding time. Don't add flavorings or table scraps to entice him—this will only make for a picky eater.

If your rottweiler is normally a good eater and suddenly stops eating, take note. He may be ill. Watch him for signs of illness (lethargy, vomiting, diarrhea, or a high temperature). If he shows any of these signs, or if he refuses to eat for more than a day, contact your veterinarian.

Poisonous Foods

You may be surprised to learn that there are foods that are perfectly fine for people but very poisonous to dogs. A list of poisonous foods you should never feed your dog include the following:

- Chocolate, especially dark chocolate
- Grapes
- Raisins
- Alcohol
- Onions

Chocolate contains theobromine, which is poisonous to dogs. Grapes and raisins contain a substance that can cause kidney failure. Alcohol, even in minute quantities, can cause alcohol poisoning. Onions are dangerous because they can lead to anemia in dogs.

Obesity

Obesity is a serious problem among pets, just as it is among humans. Obesity can affect your rottweiler's health, causing a number of obesity-related illnesses. Even puppies can be too fat. Your rottweiler should always be trim, regardless of age. Fat on a puppy is not healthy. Excessive weight can cause problems with bone and joint formation and can stress your puppy.

Determining Whether Your Rottie Is Fat

Is your rottweiler a healthy weight or a pudgy pup? You may look at the general weight guidelines for the breed to determine if your rottie is a healthy weight, but this is only a guideline and won't really determine whether he is in shape or too thin.

A much more accurate test is the rib test. Place your thumbs on your rottweiler's spine and feel his ribs with your fingers. If you cannot feel his ribs or if you have a hard time feeling them through the fat, your rottweiler is fat.

Putting Your Rottie on a Diet

If you're the not-so-proud owner of a ribless rottie, you're wondering what to do about his diet. First, talk with your veterinarian. He or she will be able to give you some recommendations regarding diet. He or she may recommend cutting back on the amount you're feeding or switching to a less active or "lite" diet. If you have difficulty limiting your rottweiler's food, try feeding a lower calorie or maintenance-type food. Eliminate all snacks, treats, and table scraps. Many dog treats are high in calories, so if you must give treats, try using ordinary dog biscuits. Exercising your rottweiler every day will also help. If you decide to exercise your rottweiler, start slowly and work up. Begin first with a short walk and increase it. Other exercises, such as playing fetch with a ball or Frisbee will help reduce the fat and increase muscle. Ⓔ

CHAPTER 8

Basic Health Care

YOUR ROTTWEILER'S GOOD HEALTH is largely dependent on you. Your veterinarian can recommend vaccinations, diet, and routine health care, but without your cooperation, your rottweiler will not be at the peak of health. Educate yourself on what is normal and abnormal with a dog. Learn the warning signs of major illnesses. You will be able to communicate more effectively with your veterinarian, and your attentiveness may someday save your dog's life.

Spaying and Neutering

Unless you're new to dog ownership, you've probably heard someone talk about spaying and neutering your pet. Maybe it was the breeder from whom you purchased your rottie or maybe it was a worker in the shelter where you found your rottie. If you haven't planned on spaying or neutering your dog, and he is a pet that you are never going to show, you should rethink your decision.

With spaying and neutering, a pet's reproductive organs are removed. There are many health benefits including the elimination or reduction of certain cancers and tumors. Contrary to common belief, spaying or neutering doesn't make your rottie fat, though you may have to cut back a bit on feeding him. It also doesn't ruin his personality. In fact, with most dogs, spaying or neutering improves your dog's personality and attentiveness.

But, if you're like many purebred owners, you may be thinking that because your rottie is purebred, you should keep him intact and maybe breed him. This is not a good idea, for several reasons:

1. Most rottweilers sold to pet homes are pet quality, at best. By breeding a pet-quality rottweiler, you're breeding mediocre puppies and contributing to the pet overpopulation.
2. Although you might have paid a lot for your rottweiler, adult purebred pet-quality dogs aren't worth a lot in the pet marketplace. Purebred rescue and shelters have adoption fees to ensure that they place the dog in a serious home and not with a wholesaler who will sell the dog to research facilities.
3. You will have to spend hundreds, if not thousands, of dollars to prove your rottweiler clear of hereditary diseases.
4. If you don't spay or neuter, you must be careful enough to prevent another dog from jumping into your backyard and mating with your rottie (or to keep your rottie from jumping out). Accidents happen all the time.
5. You run the risk of not being able to sell the puppies. How is your rottie more special than other dogs? Does he have Schutzhund, conformation, agility, herding, or obedience titles? Why would anyone want to buy your puppies when there are hundreds of other sellers?
6. You must be willing to be responsible and screen buyers and take back every rottweiler you've bred.
7. You could lose your rottweiler female if she has problems during whelping. Puppies are born dead or malformed all the time. There may be a blockage that requires veterinary intervention. Even then, whelping pups is a risky business.

When people think about keeping their dogs intact, they usually think that it is better for the dog or that they should show their kids the "miracle of birth" or some other misguided notion. The miracle of birth is best watched on a videotape—don't use your rottie as a lesson. Things go wrong; puppies and dogs die. And when the pups are older and no one wants to buy them, are you going to show your children irresponsibility by dumping them in the shelter or having them euthanized?

 **fact**

Dogs don't enjoy sex, so you aren't doing your rottie any favors. Sex is an automatic drive, and when they can't satisfy that drive, it manifests itself in bad behavior. Spaying or neutering is healthier than leaving a dog intact. So spay or neuter your rottie. It is the right thing to do.

Vaccinations

Your rottweiler needs to be vaccinated against deadly and contagious diseases such as rabies, distemper, parvovirus, and canine hepatitis to ensure his health. Diseases such as parvovirus and distemper have a mortality rate of over 50 percent.

But what vaccinations are really necessary? Over the years, new data suggests that we overvaccinate our dogs, causing autoimmune disorders and other health problems. But failing to vaccinate may cause disease to spread. It is a tough decision and one you should make with your veterinarian. Your vet should recommend vaccinations according to your location and your rottie's exposure to other dogs and canids.

Vaccines work by introducing a small amount of the disease-causing organism into a healthy dog. The dog's immune system responds by producing antibodies that are then ready to fight any subsequent infections. Sick dogs or dogs with poor immune systems should not be vaccinated without a veterinarian's approval. There are three types of vaccines available: modified live, killed, and recombinant. Modified live vaccines are genetically engineered versions of the organism's more deadly form. Modified live viruses and bacteria are able to reproduce, but they generally do no harm to a healthy dog.

The dog's body produces more antibodies to fight the infection as the modified live organism reproduces. Killed vaccines are based on the killed form of the organism. Killed vaccines do not reproduce in the dog and usually cause the body to produce fewer antibodies than the live versions. Recombinant vaccines are genetically engineered vaccines where either the virulent genes of the disease are removed or the genetic material of the disease is added to a carrier disease that will infect the dog and produce an immune response.

Rabies

Rabies is probably the best known of the contagious dog diseases due to the publicity it's gotten in Hollywood movies and in television. Rabies is a virus that attacks the brain and nervous system, causing encephalitis, and if contracted is 100 percent fatal. Any mammal can carry rabies, but it is frequently found in bats, skunks, coyotes, foxes, and raccoons. Rabies is transmitted through the infected saliva of the affected animal, usually through a bite, but occasionally through contact with wounds or by inhalation. The incubation period can be fifteen days to several months.

 **Alert!**

Rabies is still a very dangerous disease. In the United States, however, vaccinations have reduced the spread considerably. If you're ever bitten by a wild animal or a potentially rabid animal, you must be treated. However, the rabies series is no longer the ordeal it once was.

There are two forms of rabies: furious and dumb. A dog with furious rabies or "mad dog" rabies will fearlessly attack anything. Excessive drooling and paralysis characterize dumb rabies. Depending on your state health department's regulations, you must vaccinate your rottweiler once every one to three years.

Distemper

Distemper is a deadly virus that is usually fatal to puppies and older dogs that contract it. It is highly contagious and can be airborne or carried on clothing or shoes. Recovering dogs may be infectious for several months. First-stage symptoms include fever, a yellowish-gray discharge from the eyes and nose, lethargy, and appetite loss. In the second stage, the dog may have diarrhea and a dry cough. If the dog lives through these first two stages, it may appear to get well only to continue to the third and most deadly stage. The third stage occurs if there is a central nervous system involvement. The dog may develop strange twitches, convulsions, epileptic-type seizures, or paralysis. Some dogs exhibit hard-pad distemper, in which the dog's pads and nose form thick calluses. Distemper may last from ten days to several months. Vaccinations against distemper are typically given in a combination vaccine and are usually boosted yearly in adult rottweilers.

 **Fact**

A spayed or neutered dog is healthier than one that is intact. Spaying eliminates ovarian cancer and reduces the risk of mammary tumors in female dogs. Neutering eliminates testicular cancer and reduces anal tumors in male dogs.

Parvovirus

"Parvo" first appeared in 1978 and became an epidemic those first few years. It is spread through contaminated feces and can live in the soil for up to one year. Parvovirus affects all dogs, but older dogs and puppies are at high risk. Dogs that show little outward symptoms of parvovirus may be carriers and can be infectious for a long time. Parvovirus causes high fever and extreme diarrhea (often bloody), and it can affect the heart. Parvovirus has a 50-percent or even higher mortality rate among puppies. The incubation period is seven to ten days. Vaccinations against parvovirus may be given alone or in a combination vaccine and are usually boosted yearly in adult rottweilers.

Coronavirus

"Corona" is much like parvovirus as it infects the gastrointestinal system. It is spread through infected feces. The symptoms are similar to parvovirus but usually not as extreme. Veterinarians should run tests to determine if the puppy has coronavirus or parvovirus. Coronavirus may severely affect puppies, but in adult dogs the infection is usually milder than parvovirus. Parvovirus and coronavirus can infect a puppy at the same time. Vaccinations against coronavirus may be given alone or in a combination vaccine. Many boarding facilities require both bordetella and coronavirus vaccinations before accepting a dog. You should vaccinate against coronavirus if your rottweiler is exposed to large numbers of dogs, if you have a kennel, or if you have puppies. It is usually boosted yearly in adult rottweilers.

Infectious Canine Hepatitis

Canine hepatitis is a virus that is spread through infected urine. It is not related to human hepatitis. It affects the dog's liver, kidneys, and blood vessels. Recovering dogs may be infectious for months after. Its symptoms can vary from a slight fever to death. Symptoms may include eye discharge, jaundice, bloody diarrhea, hunched back, and fever. The incubation period is from four to nine days. Vaccinations against infectious canine hepatitis are typically given in a combination vaccine, and it is usually boosted yearly in adult rottweilers.

Leptospirosis

"Lepto" is a disease caused by bacteria. Rats are the main carriers through infected urine and contaminated water sources. The disease can be transmitted to humans. Dogs that recovered from leptospirosis may be infectious for months or years. Leptospirosis affects the kidneys and may also affect the liver, mouth, and tongue. Dogs that contract the disease will have a high fever and will urinate frequently. The kidneys may fail completely and require dialysis. The dog may have mouth ulcers and a thick brown substance may coat the tongue. The dog may also have jaundice-like symptoms.

 **Alert!**

Ask your veterinarian about leptospirosis. It has made a small resurgence in parts of the United States, and the current forms are more dangerous and have a higher mortality rate.

Leptospirosis usually appears between five to fifteen days after infection. Vaccinations against leptospirosis are typically given in a combination vaccine and are usually boosted yearly in adult rottweilers. Some combination vaccinations do not carry the leptospirosis vaccine because young puppies may have reactions to it.

Infectious Tracheobronchitis

Infectious tracheobronchitis, commonly known as kennel cough, is caused by different viruses and bacteria, most notably the *Bordetella bronchiseptica* bacteria, canine adenovirus types 1 and 2, and the parainfluenza virus. Breeders and veterinarians often refer to infectious tracheobronchitis as kennel cough because it is highly contagious and rapidly spreads through breeding and boarding kennels. Kennel cough can be damaging to dogs that are very old, young, or in poor health.

Dogs with kennel cough have a pronounced dry cough, which may linger for as long as two to three weeks. Complete recovery may take up to six weeks. The incubation period is between five and ten days. The vaccination against kennel cough is given once or twice yearly to adult rottweilers. However, these vaccines do not protect against all possible kennel cough viruses. Kennel cough is usually more of a nuisance than a long-lasting threat. Because there are so many viruses and bacteria that cause kennel cough, even if you vaccinate with all available kennel cough vaccinations, your rottweiler may still contract kennel cough from the viruses and bacteria there are no vaccines for.

Lyme is a tick-borne disease that originated in the Northeast and was discovered in Lyme, Connecticut, in 1975. The symptoms mimic a myriad of other diseases, with fever, lameness, fatigue, and loss of appetite being fairly common. Lyme disease is prevalent throughout the Northeast and Upper Midwest and is carried by the deer tick. In its early stages, Lyme disease is treatable with antibiotics.

Giardia

Giardia is a microscopic organism that lives in streams and lakes. It is carried through fecal matter of wildlife and is prevalent throughout the Rocky Mountains but may be found anywhere. It causes severe diarrhea, vomiting, and dehydration. Giardia is treatable with metronidazole but may take several treatments to eradicate.

Both people and dogs can contract giardia. It's prevalent in streams and in places without good filtering systems. You and your rottie should drink bottled water if you visit small towns within the Rocky Mountains, or if you run the risk of getting giardia. Small towns in the Rockies are either on well water or filter water from local streams. These municipalities often don't have the funds to completely screen their water for giardia. Locals usually have built up a tolerance for the bug, but it is unlikely you have. Hot coffee and tea are often not heated enough to kill the microorganisms either.

The Health Check

Perform regular health checks while your rottweiler is healthy so that you can identify any abnormalities quickly. A routine health check will help you monitor your dog's overall condition and determine whether a trip to the veterinarian is due. While most veterinarians perform health checks with annual vaccinations, once a year may not be enough to catch sudden conditions.

▲ Part of ensuring good health in your rottweiler pup is to make sure she gets enough exercise and rest!

Perform a health check on your rottie at least once a week. A good time to do this is while you're grooming him. If you find something that feels strange, try feeling for it on the opposite side. Normal features are usually symmetrical. If you are unsure of what is normal, ask your veterinarian. She can show you what looks and feels correct.

Checking the Head

The eyes should be clear and bright with no signs of redness. There should be no excessive discharge. There should be no yellow or pus-like discharge. Dogs do not cry, so any tears may suggest foreign bodies or irritation.

The nose should be cool and wet to the touch. There should be no discharge. A dry and hot nose may indicate fever. Also, your rottweiler should not be sneezing constantly.

 fact

> The ears should be clean and free of waxy buildup. Smell the ear. Does it smell clean or bad? Dark red or black buildup may indicate an infection or the presence of mites.

The gums should be pink and clean, not red and swollen, and the teeth should be white. Look for broken teeth and teeth that have not come in properly. If your rottweiler is over six months old, he should not have any puppy teeth. The tongue should be pink, and your rottweiler's breath should not smell bad. If it does, it may signal an underlying health problem such as gum disease.

Checking the Body

Feel down each leg. You should feel no unusual lumps or bumps. If you find a lump, check the other leg to see if the feature is symmetrical. Elbows, pads, and dewclaws can be accidentally mistaken for tumors or bumps, so if in doubt look at the lump. Move the leg slowly in its full range of motion. The movement should be fluid. If your rottweiler shows distress, or if there are any clicks, grinding, or catches, these may signal arthritis or joint problems.

Inspect the feet, both top and bottom. The skin around the toenail should be healthy, not red. The toenails should not be broken or too long. There should be no redness to the fur around the toes. If there is, your rottweiler might be licking his toes due to allergies or foreign bodies. Check the pads and in between the toes for cracks, splits, and foreign objects.

Feel along the back and ribs. You should be able to feel the spine and ribs easily. If you are unable to, your rottweiler may be overweight. He should show no sensitivity to touch along the back and the area where the kidneys are. Feel for lumps along the side. If your rottweiler hunches his back or shows sensitivity, it may indicate a more serious problem. His belly should be clean and free from dirt. Look for flea droppings and other parasites.

How to Take Your Dog's Temperature

Use an electronic thermometer that can also be used rectally. Wash the thermometer with soapy water and sterilize it with isopropyl alcohol. Use petroleum jelly as a lubricant and gently insert the thermometer into your rottweiler's rectum. Hold him quietly for about two minutes to obtain a reading. Do not allow him to sit down to keep from breaking the thermometer or pushing it farther into his rectum. Normal temperatures for rottweilers are 100.5°F to 102°F. (There are now ear thermometers for dogs that work on the same principle as the ear thermometers for humans.)

How to Give Your Dog Medicine

Most dogs hate taking medications, and rottweilers are no exception. If you must give medication in pill form, the easiest way is to slip the pill in a bit of cheese or meat and offer it to your dog. Most rotties will take the treat without stopping to chew. However, some are clever enough to eat the tidbit and spit out the pill.

 Essential

If your dog has an infection in the eye, you will likely have to treat it with an ointment. To administer eye ointment, gently pull down your rottie's lower lid and squeeze the prescribed amount into the lid.

Other times, your dog may be so sick that he may refuse the food. In this case, open your rottweiler's mouth and place the pill as far back on the tongue as possible. Close his jaws and tilt his head back, while gently stroking his throat. Most dogs will swallow, although occasionally you may one that fakes a swallow and spits out the pill. In this case, try again. There are pet pillers on the market—you insert the pill in one end and then slide the piller into your dog's mouth. With a simple push of the plunger, the pill is delivered into the correct spot. Of course, you must be somewhat proficient at getting the piller to the back of the throat in order for it to be effective.

Liquids are somewhat easier to dispense. Ask your vet for a syringe or dropper to dispense the correct amount of liquid. Slip your finger behind your dog's lower lip at the back and open a small pouch to hold the liquid. Dispense the liquid into the pouch, and let your rottweiler swallow naturally.

Internal Parasites

There are many types of internal parasites that can make your rottie very sick. Some are worms that live in the intestines and feed on the nutrition your dog needs or that actually feed on his blood. Some worms, such as heartworms, live in the heart, bloodstream, and lungs. Other internal parasites are microscopic, but these can still cause extreme diarrhea. Regardless of the type of internal parasite, your vet can help you in your fight to keep your rottie parasite-free.

Alert!

Never deworm your dog with over-the-counter dewormers. These only work on specific types of worms and will do no good if you treat for the wrong type of worm. Since all dewormers are poisons, it is best to have your vet diagnose the type of infestation and then recommend the appropriate dewormer.

Worms

A dog or puppy becomes infected when he accidentally ingests the worm's eggs. The most common source of contamination is fecal material. However, your rottweiler can also contract worms from eating raw meat from infected animals such as rodents, game, or farm animals. Fleas carry tapeworms that, when accidentally ingested, can infest your rottweiler. The most common worms are roundworms, hookworms, tapeworms, and whipworms.

Roundworms, and to a lesser extent, tapeworms, can infect people through the oral-fecal route. Children have contracted round-worms, but because people aren't the normal host for them, the roundworms migrate to places like eyes, causing blindness. It is very important to keep your dogs worm-free.

 **Essential**

Although worms are common in puppies, worms will make your rottweiler sick. When you take your rottweiler to the veterinarian, ask him if you should bring a fecal sample. Your veterinarian may want to run a fecal test and check for parasites.

If your rottweiler has diarrhea, bloating, weight loss (or is not gaining weight), bloody stools, anemia, or rice-like flecks around the anus, have your veterinarian run a fecal test to look for worms. Rottweilers that scoot on their bottoms are more likely to have impacted anal sacs than worms, but you should have your veterinarian check for worms anyway.

Roundworms

Roundworms (*Toxocara canis*) are the most common worms. Your rottweiler may have been infected with roundworms even before he was born! Roundworms lie dormant in a female dog's body and start migrating to the puppies when the female becomes pregnant. Roundworms can even infect the mother's milk, and the puppies can pick them up while nursing. Other avenues for trans-mission include fecal matter.

Contracting roundworms is not a statement of the breeder's care. If your rottweiler's mother has ever had roundworms during her life, your puppy has probably contracted them through her. However, the breeder should deworm the puppies.

Roundworm infestation can be serious in puppies and in old and debilitated dogs. Roundworms feed off the nutrition intended for your rottie. A puppy that is infested may have a pot belly, may lose weight, and may have a poor coat. Other signs include vomiting, diarrhea, and a garlic odor to the breath. Take your puppy and a fecal sample to the vet. Roundworms can be quite serious and can kill a puppy.

Hookworms

Hookworms (*Ancylostoma caninum*) are smaller than roundworms and feed in the small intestine from your rottweiler's blood. Dogs contract hookworms either through skin penetration (they can burrow into a dog's skin) or through the mother's milk. Severe infestations can be life threatening and can cause severe anemia. Diarrhea, weight loss, and lethargy are signs of hookworm infestation.

 **Fact**

Whipworms (*Trichuris vulpis*) are difficult to diagnose because they don't always produce eggs in fecal matter. These worms feed on blood in the large intestine. Like hookworms, these worms can be serious and cause severe anemia. Dogs become infested by eating something in contaminated soil.

Tapeworms

Tapeworms (*Dipylidium caninum*) are long, flat worms that may infest your rottweiler's intestines. These worms may break off and be excreted in his feces. They look like grains of rice in the feces or around the dog's anus. Fleas commonly carry tapeworms. Your rottweiler may swallow a flea, thus becoming infested with tapeworms. Other modes of transmission include raw game meat. Some dogs catch and eat mice or other rodents that carry tapeworms.

Heartworm

Heartworm is a deadly internal parasite that lives in the heart, bloodstream, and lungs. Mosquitoes carry heartworm from an infected dog to others by injecting the larvae into the dog as it feeds on the dog's blood. Heartworm is prevalent in most of the continental United States. Dogs in warmer climates need to be on heartworm preventive year round, while dogs from northern states must be on a preventive during the spring and summer months.

Your veterinarian should test your rottie for adult heartworm before putting him on a preventive. If your rottie has a heartworm infestation, it should be treated before he is put on a preventive. Heartworm treatment used to be very dangerous, requiring the veterinarians to administer an intravenous arsenic-based solution. There is a new heartworm treatment that veterinarians administer intramuscularly. This new treatment is less risky and has fewer side effects. If your rottweiler has heartworms, be sure your veterinarian is using a newer treatment than the old arsenic-based treatment. Heartworm treatment is still risky and expensive, so it is better to prevent heartworm than treat it.

 Fact

Heartworm is spreading through the United States. As a result of our mobile society, places that didn't have heartworms even ten years ago now have it. Ask your vet what the incidence of heartworms is in your area.

There are many excellent heartworm preventives. Most available are chewable and are given monthly. Do not use the old daily heartworm preventive as it is less effective when not administered properly. Some monthly heartworm preventives now also control other internal parasites.

Giardia and Coccidia

Other internal parasites include microscopic organisms that can cause diarrhea and vomiting. The most common of these organisms are giardia and coccidia.

Giardia is a common microorganism that lives in streams. Metronidazole is the common method of treatment for giardia. Your veterinarian will have to run a test on a stool sample to determine if your rottie has giardia and may prescribe medication to treat it. Sometimes giardia comes back, and you may need several treatments to thoroughly eliminate it. There is a new vaccine on the market that protects dogs from giardia.

Coccidia is a common microorganism in puppy mills and large kennels. This protozoa is generally associated with unsanitary conditions. However, as the disease is often carried by birds, reputable breeders may have coccidia in their kennels. Once it is introduced into an environment, it is very difficult to eliminate.

Symptoms of coccidia include diarrhea and vomiting. Your rottie may contract coccidia through ingesting feces or licking a contaminated surface. Pick up all feces and use an ammonia-based pine cleaner to kill the microorganisms. Bleach will not kill coccidia; only strong ammonia-based cleaners will be effective. The treatment of choice for coccidia is Albon, which is available through your vet.

External Parasites

External parasites are nasty critters that will make your rottie miserable. But they're not just a nuisance, they're a health threat both to you and your rottie. For instance, fleas can carry diseases such as bubonic plague, and ticks can carry diseases such as Lyme disease and Rocky Mountain spotted fever.

Fleas

Fleas are black, red, or brown, hard-shelled insects that feed on blood. They can make your rottweiler miserable. Worse yet, some dogs become allergic to the flea saliva and may suffer flea-bite dermatitis. Fleas can carry bubonic plague and other diseases. They can also carry tapeworms that can infect your rottweiler.

 **Alert!**

Do not use flea collars, as they are not effective. Your rottweiler can chew and swallow collars like these, and they will poison him. Ultrasonic collars, garlic, brewer's yeast, and other herbal remedies are also not proven effective.

Common flea feeding areas are anywhere that there is tender skin. Ears, belly, groin, and pelvic areas are prime flea spots. Look for flea feces—they appear as dark grains that turn red when wet. You can comb through your rottie's coat with a flea comb to search for the pests. Fleas do not fly, but they can jump great distances. Most areas in the United States are flea-prone, with the exception of those that are at high altitudes, very cold, or very hot and dry.

Consult your veterinarian for a good system to combat or prevent flea infestation. Many manufacturers have created fleas systems that are intended to work together for use on your dog, in your house, and in your yard. Products are available from your veterinarian or by mail order. These can break the fleas' reproductive cycle and reduce the amount of insecticides needed. There are also many good systemic flea control systems you can administer topically.

Regardless of how you intend to fight fleas, always read the warning labels for any product you plan to use. All insecticides are poisons that can harm you or your rottweiler if used improperly. Always follow the product's instructions. Some medications may interact with the insecticides, so always consult your veterinarian if your dog is on a medication. Never mix insecticides together, and be careful using different insecticides that may interact. Do not use them on puppies or sick dogs without first consulting your veterinarian. If you have questions concerning the possible interaction or poisonings, consult the hot line number on the product, your veterinarian, or the poison control center.

 **fact**

The deer ticks that carry Lyme disease are very small—so small (about the size of a pinhead) that you might miss them. Their nymphs (larvae) can also carry the disease and are practically invisible to the naked eye.

Ticks

Ticks carry numerous, potentially fatal diseases such as Rocky Mountain spotted fever, Lyme disease, and ehrlichiosis. If you find a tick on your rottweiler, wear disposable latex gloves and do not handle the tick to avoid contamination. Use a good tick insecticide approved for use on dogs, and treat the tick and area around it. After a few minutes, you can try to remove the tick. Use tweezers to grasp the tick close to the skin and pull out slowly. If the tick's head or legs do not retract, do not pull the tick off. The tick bite can become severely infected if you leave the head or legs in the skin. Wait for the tick to drop off and dispose of it.

There are tick collars on the market that can be very effective; most are available through your veterinarian and some mail-order pet-supply houses. However, if your rottweiler becomes sleepy after you put the collar on, remove it immediately and take him to the veterinarian. Sleepiness is a sign of an allergic reaction.

CHAPTER 9

Basic Grooming

WHEN A ROTTIE IS CLEAN and his coat is shiny and well cared for, there isn't a more beautiful dog. But grooming your rottweiler isn't just for aesthetics. Grooming is a necessary part of caring for his health. Rotties are easy to groom. Some may say that they're "wash and wear" dogs. They don't need clipping or expensive scissoring to have a beautiful coat. But there's still work to be done, and if you don't have time for grooming, you might want to consider other options.

Use a Groomer or Do It Yourself?

Considering that the rottweiler is easy to maintain, you may think that a groomer is a bit of a luxury. But a low-maintenance coat doesn't mean a no-maintenance coat. Rotties are double-coated, and they shed once or twice a year. They require a minimum of a once-a-week brushing and a bath once a month or when they get dirty. If you are too busy to keep up with a grooming schedule, you might want to consider hiring a professional groomer. Groomers charge between $20 and $40, depending on what you want done.

To find a good groomer, ask your dog-owning friends for recommendations or contact your vet. Many vets have groomers on-site. If you still can't find a good groomer nearby, contact the National Dog Groomers Association of America at ☎(412) 962-2711 and ask for members in your area.

Before you make an appointment with a groomer, you'll want to ask if she's comfortable working with rottweilers. You'll also want to find out if the groomer uses tranquilizers. Some groomers do, and if your rottie has epilepsy or is particularly sensitive to medications, you may wish to look elsewhere. Some groomers use muzzles with aggressive or hard-to-handle dogs. If your rottie is old, you may wish to ask what provisions the groomer makes to see that an older dog is comfortable. Ask the groomer what services she'll perform and how much she charges. Some will only brush and bathe, but others will clean ears, clip toenails, and express anal sacs. It is important to know ahead of time.

 **Essential**

Your rottie should also be comfortable with strangers handling him. If he is aggressive toward strangers, you may want to reconsider your choice to take him to a groomer and groom him yourself until you can properly socialize him.

Visit the groomer. The grooming room should be clean and free of dirt (though if she has been busy, there might be hair and water on the floor). If the groomer uses crate dryers, she should check on the dogs frequently—leaving a dog in a crate dryer unattended can be fatal. Both the groomer and staff should be pleasant. They should handle the dogs with kindness and care, even if the dog becomes agitated. You should leave the groomer's place feeling as though this is a good place to bring your rottweiler.

Grooming Supplies

Regardless of whether you decide to use a groomer, you should still have grooming implements so you can groom your rottie yourself. These should include the following:

- Slicker brush
- Curry brush or Zoom Groom
- Short comb
- Flea comb
- Dog toenail clippers
- Styptic powder
- Dog shampoo and conditioner
- Otic solution
- Cotton balls
- Toothbrush for dogs
- Toothpaste for dogs

Two useful pieces of equipment are a hair dryer for dogs and a grooming table. Dog hair dryers use forced air, but they have no heat, so they won't burn your rottie's skin. Grooming tables are great for you because they help prevent injury by raising the dog to a manageable height.

 **Alert!**

Don't use shampoo or conditioner for humans on dogs. They aren't correctly pH balanced for a dog's skin and can dry out your rottie's fur. Never use human toothpaste on dogs. The fluoride in human toothpaste is poisonous to dogs. Use only toothpaste specially formulated for dogs.

Brushing and Combing

You need to brush and comb your rottie at least once a week. If you're planning on bathing your rottie, you will first have to brush and comb him out to remove any dead hair and dirt. Brushing and combing stimulates the hair and skin, making it healthy and distributing the skin's natural oils.

Start with the curry brush or Zoom Groom to clean the dust and dirt out of his coat. Use a short comb to comb through the coat once. Then, use a slicker brush to brush against the grain of your rottie's coat to loosen and remove any dead hair. Brush the hair back in place.

◀ Rottweilers' appearances reflect their calm, confident nature.

Removing Mats

Because of their short coats, rotties generally don't have trouble with mats. However, if your rottie hasn't been brushed in a while or has gotten something stuck in his fur, use a detangling solution and a comb or mat breaker to gently remove the mats. If the mats are severe, take your rottie to a groomer to have the mats removed. Sometimes mats have to be shaved out with electronic clippers.

Bathing

Bathe your rottie whenever he's dirty with a good shampoo that's pH balanced especially for dogs. Use tepid water. Water that is comfortable for you may be too hot for him, so lukewarm water is best. Most dogs hate bathing and will do anything they can to avoid it. Some pet-supply stores carry a suction cup that clips onto your rottweiler's collar and attaches to the tub's side. This works if he doesn't pull too hard—otherwise, you may find him by the bathroom door begging to get out. If you have a sturdy handle in your bathroom, such as a handhold, you can tie his leash to it and clip his collar to it to hold him in place. If you do this, never leave your rottie unattended. He could accidentally strangle himself.

 Essential

Never bathe a rottweiler that hasn't been brushed out first or one that has mats. You need to comb out the dead hair and remove the mats before you bathe or you will have a worse problem.

After shampooing your rottweiler, follow up with a conditioner especially made for dogs. Be certain to rinse well. Shampoo and conditioner residue will collect dirt faster and can dry out and irritate your dog's skin.

Bathing Essentials

When you bathe your rottie, you'll want to bathe him in a draft-free area. During the wintertime, this means indoors, which may make washing interesting. Once you've thoroughly rinsed him, pat him down with towels and keep him warm until he dries. If you have a blow dryer made for dogs, you can use that on him. Never use a blow dryer made for humans. The hot air will burn your rottie.

The Dog Wash

There are now places where you can wash your dog for under $10. Some are in pet-supply stores but others are actual businesses that offer special areas for washing your dog. The places supply the soap, towels, and grooming implements as well as bathing tubs, grooming tables, and dog hair dryers. They are a low-cost alternative to paying a groomer and a low-mess alternative to bathing your rottweiler in your house.

Cleaning Ears

Dogs with ears that droop like the rottweiler's tend to be more prone to ear infections. You need to keep your rottie's ears clean and sweet-smelling by cleaning them when they're dirty or once a week.

Use a mild otic solution made for cleaning dogs' ears. Avoid solutions with medications and mite treatments as these can cause irritation. If you suspect an infection or mites, have your veterinarian look at your dog's ears. Squeeze a little otic solution into his ears and gently massage them. Use sterile gauze or sponges to wipe out the excess.

Your rottie may have an ear infection or mites if you observe the following:

- Ears are foul smelling.
- Rottie paws or scratches his ears or shakes his head.
- Ears have an excessive red, black, or waxy buildup.
- Ears are crusty or red.

If your rottie has any of these symptoms, you should take him to the vet for the appropriate treatment.

Clipping Toenails

Most dog owners would rank clipping toenails right up there with root canals and tooth extractions. And with good reason. Most dogs hate getting their toenails clipped, and rotties are no exception.

What makes matters worse is that rotties have black toenails, which makes it impossible to see the quick. Consequently, inexperienced rottie owners accidentally cut the quick, which firmly cements a profound hatred of toenail clipping within their rottie's mind.

 **Question?**

What is the quick?
The quick is the blood supply for the nail. It is very sensitive and if cut will bleed a lot. If you accidentally cut into it, not only will you have a mess, but you'll also have a rottweiler that will never want you to touch his feet again.

There are two types of nail clippers: the guillotine variety and the scissors type. Both are good if they have sharp blades. The scissors type sometimes has a safety stop that helps gauge a safe amount of nail to snip off.

Handling His Feet

Your rottie may not wish you to handle his feet at first. In this case, get him used to your holding his feet by picking up one foot at a time and letting it go. Give him a treat when you're done. Practice this often, and slowly increase the amount of time you hold his foot. When you finally can hold his foot long enough to clip his nails, try it.

Trimming Your Rottie's Toenails

Hold your rottie's foot and snip off a small portion of the nail. If you have a safety stop, use that as a guide. Clip each toenail, and don't forget to clip the dewclaws if he has them. Give him a treat afterward. You'll need to clip his toenails once a week.

If there's a trick to snipping black toenails, it is taking only a little bit at a time. Stop if the nail feels spongy or if your rottie acts uncomfortable. If you do hit the quick, pack the nail with styptic powder to stop the bleeding. Another device, which costs more than the clippers, is a nail grinder. Dogs that dislike the clippers sometimes tolerate the grinder far better.

The quick grows as the nail grows. If you don't cut your rottie's toenails, the quick will be correspondingly long. The way to reduce the toenail and shrink the quick is to keep the nails cut short just before the quick and let the quick recede. After a few days, the quick will have receded and you can trim some more nail.

If you're unsure about clipping your rottie's nails, ask your vet or groomer to show you how to do it.

Dental Hygiene

Dogs don't get cavities the way we do, but they can have dental problems, such as tartar buildup and gum disease. This is why it is very important for you to brush your rottie's teeth at least once a week, but preferably daily.

Brushing Your Rottie's Teeth

Some dogs dislike having their mouths handled. If your rottie doesn't like you touching his mouth, you can start with just flipping his cheek flap up and then praising him and giving him a treat. Do this several times a day so that he becomes used to your touching his lips.

 Alert!

If your rottie starts chewing on things he's not supposed to, consider making an appointment with the vet to see if there's something wrong with his teeth. Dogs can't tell you it hurts, so they try to alleviate the pain by chewing.

Once he is used to your touching his mouth, get a washcloth and wet the corner. Hold the washcloth so that your index finger is on the corner. Flip up your rottie's lip and gently touch his gums with the corner of the washcloth. Give him a treat. Do this several times a day and gradually lengthen the time you touch his gums with the washcloth. If he tolerates that, try gently massaging his gums with the wet washcloth.

Once he lets you rub his gums, it is time for a toothbrush and toothpaste. Use a toothbrush specially made for pets (some slip over the fingers) and use special pet toothpaste. (Don't use human toothpaste because it is toxic to your rottie.) Most pet toothpastes are either malt or chicken flavored, so it'll be quite a treat. Brush his teeth in a circular motion, and don't forget to brush the gums as well. Your rottie doesn't have to rinse and spit.

The Doggy Dentist

If you care for your rottie's teeth, it is less likely he'll have to visit the doggie dentist. Still, a variety of factors are involved in determining whether your rottie will have healthy teeth. These include:

- **Genetics**—Heredity plays a role in whether a dog has good teeth.
- **Diet**—A good diet can prevent some dental disease.
- **Disease**—Some diseases can actually weaken the enamel on the tooth.
- **Accidents or fights**—Teeth can be broken in an accident or a dogfight.
- **Dental care**—Brushing your rottie's teeth can keep the doggy dentist at bay.

Dental Problems

Even if your rottie has the best of teeth, you should still be on the lookout for dental problems. Signs of a possible dental problem include these:

- Lack of appetite
- Foul breath
- Swollen gums
- Change in chewing or eating habits

- Sudden grumpiness
- Red gums
- Chipped or broken tooth

Talk to your vet about dental hygiene and your rottie. He or she may be able to make recommendations for diet and brushing teeth.

Anal Sacs

Anal sacs, or the anal glands, are two glands that sit at the four and eight o'clock positions around a dog's anus. They are filled with stinky fluid and usually express themselves when a dog defecates. (Dogs can express their anal sacs when they're fearful or nervous.) However, they can become full or impacted.

 **Essential**

Dogs who scoot along the ground or bite their rumps may have full anal glands. If you decide to empty them, do it while you bathe your rottie. These glands can really squirt, and they're foul-smelling.

To express the anal glands, get some paper towels and fold them up into an absorbent square. Place them over your dog's anus and press at the four and eight o'clock positions. Keep your face away from there as it can really squirt. Throw away the paper towel and wash your rottie thoroughly. If your rottie still has problems with his anal sacs, he may have an impacted anal gland and your vet may have to clear it.

Removing Skunk Odor

If your rottie is skunked, you may have heard that using tomato juice will clean it right up. The tomato-juice myth has been around for a long time, even though it doesn't work. The truth is that the person who is bathing the dog in tomato juice gets used to the skunk smell (their olfactory senses have been overloaded) and eventually can't smell it. Other home remedies, such as douche or dandruff shampoos, won't remove the smell either. Instead, purchase a good commercial skunk odor remover or use this do-it-yourself remedy:

1 quart hydrogen peroxide
¼ cup baking soda
1 tsp dog shampoo

Mix it together, and wash your rottie with it. Be careful and keep the solution out of his eyes. Rinse thoroughly. Throw out any leftover solution because it can explode if kept in a container. This really works, and he might end up smelling better than before he got skunked.

 **Alert!**

Skunks are carriers of rabies. If your rottie catches and kills one, you may have more trouble than just the skunk odor. Handle the dead skunk with rubber gloves and bag it. Have the state health department check it for rabies, and talk to your vet about getting a rabies booster for your rottie.

Removing Sticky Substances

Depending on the substance, you can try corn oil to loosen a sticky substance and wash it clean from your rottie. Otherwise, if it is tar or a petroleum-based substance, you will have to use a degreaser such as Dawn dishwashing liquid, GOOP, or Orange Power. If you're worried about the chemicals, be aware that many dishwashing detergents with degreasers are actually excellent at removing petroleum products. They're often used on seabirds caught in oil slicks. Dawn is the mildest and is very effective. The two others mentioned are excellent at removing grease, but they are irritants. Be sure to bathe your rottie and wash all traces of the substance from his coat and skin. ⓔ

Common Illnesses and Injuries

EVEN WITH THE BEST CARE, your rottie will still occasionally become sick. Dogs are prone to illnesses and accidents just as people are. In this chapter, you'll learn when you can take care of your dog for minor problems like stomach upsets and when the illness is important enough to take your dog to the vet.

When to Visit a Vet

Your rottweiler is feeling under the weather. Perhaps he's not playing or has thrown up his food. Should you take him to the vet, or will he get over it? After all, you don't want to go when there's no need.

Most ailments such as a bout of diarrhea or vomiting may be nothing more than a stomach bug, or perhaps your rottie has eaten something that disagreed with him. But there's really no way to know if there is something more serious happening unless you do take him to a vet.

The following are problems for which you do need to take your dog to the vet:

- He has a temperature over 102.5°F.
- Rottie doesn't eat for more than one day; sudden change in eating habits, either becoming voracious or not willing to eat at all; excessive thirst; or sudden gain or loss in weight.

- Rottie has diarrhea or vomiting for more than twelve hours; has diarrhea or vomiting with fever or projectile vomits; diarrhea is bloody, black, or mucus-filled; vomit is black or contains blood; rottie starts showing signs of dehydration; straining to urinate or defecate; or dark or bloody urine.
- Rottie is bleeding or has unusual discharge from mouth, anus, or genitals.
- Unexplained lump.
- Excessive itching, scratching, or biting; or hair loss or bald patches.
- Limping; lethargy, stumbling, or inability to move properly; or broken bones.
- Puncture wounds, deep cuts, and other wounds that will require suturing; or weeping wounds or wounds with pus.
- Sudden unexplained behavior: becomes aggressive or reticent if touched; whimpers or looks distressed; or incontinence, sudden loss of housetraining.
- Seizures; or coughing, choking, or gagging.
- Broken or cracked tooth.

Many of these problems are serious or even deadly. The main thing to remember is that if your rottie shows a sudden change in his behavior, or if there is a sudden change in weight, eating, or drinking, it is time for a trip to the veterinarian. Many problems are biological in nature and should not be summarily dismissed as behavioral.

For example, if your rottweiler growls or snaps when you touch him on his hindquarters, it might not mean he's ill tempered. It might mean he has arthritis or hip dysplasia and the pain is causing him to behave aggressively. Some problems aren't quite as obvious. Your rottie might sneak off to urinate in an unused room. You might think he's marking or forgotten his housetraining, but it could also be a urinary tract infection, kidney stones, or another potentially dangerous medical condition.

Allergies

Achoo! Rotties suffer from allergies and intolerances now more than ever. Some people cite our environment as the cause since we're bombarded with toxins and pollutants. Others think it might be the indiscriminant breeding rottweilers suffered during the 1980s and 1990s. Sneezing is one component of allergies, but allergies take other forms as well. In your rottweiler, allergies may appear as food allergies or contact allergies.

Dietary allergies are becoming common among dogs. They're a bit tricky to diagnose. Your vet will recommend a hypoallergenic diet for several weeks. This diet usually has a novel protein source—that is, a protein source that dogs generally don't eat, such as fish or venison. (Contrary to popular belief, lamb is *not* a hypoallergenic meat.) They may have an unusual carbohydrate source too, such as potatoes or barley. After your rottie is on this diet for several weeks, you add the potential problem ingredients to determine what the allergy is. Some dog owners are so relieved to have their dogs free from the allergy that they just keep them on the hypoallergenic diet.

 **Question?**

Is a hypoallergenic diet any better for your rottie?
This food isn't better than any other in terms of nutrition, and if your rottweiler isn't allergic to his current food, he doesn't need to eat a hypoallergenic diet.

Contact allergies occur when the dog comes in contact with something external to his body. Some contact allergies are apparent, but some aren't as easy to diagnose. For example, if your dog's skin looks irritated and is itchy after using a particular shampoo, you might guess that the dog is allergic to a chemical in that shampoo. However, you might not know why your dog's nose and face are swollen and irritated. Many dogs are allergic to plastic or rubber and may react to the plastic bowls you feed them out of. Most contact allergy diagnoses are based on the owner's observations.

Skin Problems

Skin problems can range anywhere from simple cuts to dangerous infections. Some you can treat on your own, but many require help from your veterinarian. If at any time you're not sure what you're doing, consult with your vet.

Cuts and Scrapes

Unless particularly deep, most cuts and scrapes will heal without much attention. Clean the wound with a mild solution of betadine or hydrogen peroxide mixed with water. You can use a good triple antibiotic ointment (available at the drugstore) for the cut and keep an eye on it to make certain it heals. Have your vet look at the wound if there is any redness, swelling, pus, or other sign of infection. Keep the wound clean. If you must, bandage it with a sterile wound dressing and gauze (be certain not to get the gauze too tight or you may constrict circulation). Change the dressings daily or when they get dirty or wet.

 **Fact**

Sometimes your rottweiler will develop a lump around a vaccination injection site. If so, notify your vet. He may want to have you watch the injection site closely or put your rottie on medication.

You can prevent your rottweiler from chewing or licking his bandages either with a bitter substance (like Bitter Apple) or with one of those plastic Elizabethan-style collars. The Elizabethan collar (available through your vet) is cone-shaped and prevents a dog from chewing or worrying at his bandages. Most dogs (and dog owners) find these collars disconcerting, but with some help from their owner, they can eat, drink, and even sleep with an Elizabethan collar on.

Excessive Licking

If your rottie has been licking an area excessively, you'll see where the fur has been chewed or the area has turned red. The area where your rottie is licking is usually a source of irritation. It could be from allergies, dry skin, yeast or fungal infection, foreign body, mites, flea allergy dermatitis, injury, or a skin condition. If you look at the place where your rottie is licking and see no foreign body, take him to the vet to have the problem looked at. Your vet can prescribe the appropriate treatment.

 **Alert!**

Dogs have a different chemical makeup than humans. Never give your rottweiler acetaminophen (the active ingredient in Tylenol) or ibuprofen (Motrin, Advil). Both are very dangerous to dogs and should never be given at human dosages.

Flea Allergy Dermatitis

Flea allergy dermatitis, or fleabite dermatitis, can cause itchy skin. With flea allergy dermatitis, the dog becomes allergic to the flea saliva. Eliminating fleas from your rottweiler and your home will solve the problem and provide welcome relief. Your veterinarian can prescribe medications to alleviate the itching.

Foxtails

Foxtails, or grass awns, are seeds from grass-like plants. They have a sharp, burrowing head with a tail that looks like a fox's tail (hence the name). These seeds have a nasty habit of getting into your rottie's fur and ears. With each movement, they burrow into the dog's skin.

Check your rottie thoroughly for burrs and foxtails after he's been outside. Be sure to check his ears, too. Foxtails will bury themselves deeply into a dog's skin. They can cause abscesses and can even enter organs.

Hot Spots (Moist Dermatitis)

Hot spots are areas of moist dermatitis (skin inflammation) that may become infected. The symptoms are reddening skin, missing hair, and oozing wound-like lesions. Allergies, matted fur, or some other form of irritation frequently causes them. Shave or clip all hair surrounding the hot spot and clean twice daily with a solution of 10 percent betadine and 90 percent water. If the hot spots are too painful, infected, or extensive, your veterinarian may have to anesthetize your rottweiler to shave them and prescribe corticosteroids and antibiotics.

 **Essential**

Your rottie could have itchy skin for a number of reasons. If your dog's coat is dull and dry, try adding 1 to 2 teaspoons of canola oil to your dog's meal once a day and a hardboiled egg three times a week. If your rottie's coat remains dry and brittle or if it is thinning, consider having him tested for hypothyroidism.

Lumps Under the Skin

Most lumps are usually benign. However, you should show any lump or bump to your veterinarian. Lumps that are oozing, red, dark-colored, irregular in size and shape, or swift-growing may be serious. If your female rottweiler has lumps on her mammary glands, they may be cancerous mammary tumors requiring surgery. A large doughy lump on the stomach might be a hernia that your veterinarian may have to fix.

Rapidly growing lumps may be a form of abscess or infection. Abscesses occur when foreign bodies enter the skin (such as foxtails), or an injury closes with bacteria inside. Abscesses are serious. Your veterinarian must drain the abscess and prescribe antibiotics. Do not attempt to drain the abscess yourself or the wound may become even more infected.

A lump or bump doesn't necessarily mean cancer. An unexplained lump or bump may be a cyst, a fatty tumor, an abscess, or other cause. Regardless, always have your vet check out any lump you find.

Mange

Mange mites can cause itching and hair loss. The two common types of mange are sarcoptic and demodectic. Sarcoptic mange causes intense itching. Demodectic causes severe hair loss. Demodectic mange is often caused by a weakened immune system. It can be seen in puppies and will often clear itself up. Both must be diagnosed through skin scrapings and treated through a veterinarian. Over-the-counter remedies seldom work.

Ringworm

Ringworm can cause hair loss, leaving round patches of scaly skin. It is contagious to humans and other animals, so use disposable latex gloves when treating it. Use a mixture of 90 percent water and 10 percent betadine (available from your veterinarian) to treat the skin. Shampoos and soaps containing iodine work well. Your veterinarian can prescribe oral medication for chronic or widespread ringworm.

 Fact

You may be surprised to learn that ringworm isn't a worm at all but a fungus. It is highly contagious to cats and people with lowered immune systems (such as the elderly and children).

Gastric Problems

Some gastric problems, such as diarrhea and vomiting, can be mild or severe. Some you can treat; others require veterinary intervention. Always be mindful that many conditions can lead to dehydration, which is very serious. Never allow a condition to go longer than a day without at least talking to your vet.

Bad Breath

"Dog breath" has been the butt of jokes ever since people and dogs have been together. However, bad breath isn't a laughing matter. It can be a sign of a more serious problem, such as gum disease, gastric problems, or maybe a rotting tooth. It can also suggest a more serious internal health problem, such as cancer. A trip to the vet is in order. If bad breath is simply a matter of dental hygiene, brush your rottie's teeth regularly (as described in Chapter 9).

Diarrhea and Vomiting

Changes in diet, overeating, strange water, and nervousness can cause diarrhea, but so can parvovirus, internal parasites, rancid food, allergies, and other serious ailments. If your rottweiler is dehydrated, has a fever (temperature over 102°F), or has extreme or bloody diarrhea, take him to your veterinarian as soon as possible.

 **Alert!**

Know the signs of dehydration. If you pull up on the skin on the back of your rottweiler's neck and it "melts" back or stays there instead of snapping back, your rottie is dehydrated. Other signs include sticky lips and gums.

If your rottweiler has mild diarrhea (soft stools—not liquid and without mucus) and is not dehydrated or vomiting, you can give him a tablespoon of a kaolin product (like Kaopectate) or one made with bismuth subsalicylate (such as Pepto-Bismol). Withhold his next meal to see if the diarrhea improves. Encourage him to drink water or an unflavored pediatric electrolyte solution. If there is no diarrhea or vomiting, you can feed him a mixture of boiled hamburger and rice at the next meal. If your rottweiler's condition does not improve or becomes worse, contact your veterinarian.

Dogs vomit for a variety of reasons. Dogs will sometimes eat grass and vomit. Dogs also vomit as a reaction to obstructions, an enlarged esophagus, parvovirus and other serious illnesses, allergies, or rancid food. If your rottweiler vomits more than once or twice, projectile vomits, starts becoming dehydrated, has severe diarrhea along with vomiting, has a fever (temperature over 102°F), or retches without vomiting, take him to the veterinarian immediately.

Lack of Appetite

Contrary to popular belief, missing a meal or two isn't healthy for a dog. Missing a meal suggests that something might be wrong. If your rottie has missed a meal and shows no other symptoms, watch him carefully and feed him at his normal time (no snacks!). If he eats at his next meal, then it is unlikely there was anything wrong.

However, if your rottie misses an entire day's worth of food or misses a meal and has other symptoms, you should take him to the vet for a checkup. A dog that normally eats well and then suddenly stops eating is definitely a cause for concern.

Feet and Legs

Your rottie may occasionally have problems with his feet or legs. Limping is usually the first sign something is amiss, but not always. Your rottie could be tender in areas, too. It's very important to examine your rottweiler often so you will be able to find problems before they get out of control.

Broken Toenails

Your rottweiler may experience cracked or broken toenails, especially if you allow them to grow too long. Trim the toenail and file off any rough edges if the toenail has broken below the quick (the blood supply to the nail). If the nail is bleeding, you can stop the bleeding with styptic powder, silver nitrate, or an electric nail cauterizer available through pet mail-order catalogues. You can then paint the nail with a skin bond agent, available from your veterinarian or through veterinary supply houses. Keep your rottweiler's toenails short so that he won't snag them on something and tear them. Torn toenails can be painful.

Limping

Limping can be the sign of a muscular strain or sprain. It might be a burr or something caught in his pads. It can also be a sign of serious injury, cancer, arthritis, or a tick-borne disease, such as Lyme disease. If your rottie just suddenly starts to limp, you may want to gently check his foot—assuming he will let you—and see if you can find anything stuck in or between his pads. Gently feel along his leg to see if you can detect swelling or tenderness. If the limp is minor, you may wish to see if rest will improve it. However, if the limp does not go away, is severe, or if it is chronic, you will need to have a veterinarian look at it.

Incontinence

Incontinence is generally a sign of a more serious problem such as a bladder or urinary tract infection or bladder stones. Have your vet examine your dog to determine the cause of incontinence. Occasionally, spayed female dogs "dribble," and they may require medication to correct this. Ⓔ

CHAPTER 11

Emergencies

LIFE-THREATENING EMERGENCIES seldom occur during a veterinarian's normal office hours. Should your rottweiler become sick or injured, having a first-aid kit and emergency numbers handy may save his life. In all emergencies, obtain veterinary treatment as soon as possible. The following information will help you care for your rottweiler in an emergency. It is intended as a guide only. It is not a substitute for professional emergency veterinary care.

Identification

One emergency dog owners are never prepared for is a lost or stolen dog. It is vitally important that your rottie have two forms of identification: one on his collar and a permanent form. There are two types of permanent forms of identification: microchip and tattoo. Regardless of the type of permanent identification you use, you must have it registered with a national registry so if your rottie is ever lost or stolen, you can identify him.

Tags are a cheap form of identification. You can pick up tags through mail-order catalogues, on the Internet, or at large pet-supply stores for $4 to $8. No dog should be without up-to-date tags.

Tattoos are a permanent form of identification, costing between $5 and $25 to do, not including the registration fee. Groomers, veterinarians, and other dog professionals can tattoo your rottie. Be sure to have the tattoo placed inside the thigh. The tattoo is useless unless it is registered with a national database for pet recovery.

 Essential

Have all your papers (AKC, health records, and so on) in one place in case there is ever an emergency. You never know when you may need to produce his vaccination records or other information. Also, keep a good photograph of your rottie in case he's lost and you have to show people what he looks like.

Microchips are a permanent form of identification, costing between $25 and $50 plus registration fee. There are several forms of microchips, but a popular one is the "Home Again" chip offered through the AKC. The microchip is useless unless it is registered with a national database for pet recovery.

While having identification on your rottweiler is important if he accidentally gets out, it's also important if you're separated from him in an accident or disaster. This is why your rottweiler should have two forms of identification on him at all times.

First-Aid Kits

Being prepared for an emergency is extremely important. Quite often being prepared is the difference between a good or disastrous outcome. The more prepared you are, the less likely you'll panic or freeze when the emergency occurs.

Have several first-aid kits available. Make one for home, one for traveling or the car, and maybe one to bring with you camping or to dog shows. Keep them well stocked, and be certain to buy more supplies after you use them. You can use the recommendations here for what to put in your first-aid kit, or you can ask your veterinarian.

There are some ready-made first-aid kits available for dogs, but they may or may not be complete. Human first-aid kits will have some medicines (such as acetaminophen and ibuprofen) you can't give your rottweiler.

 **Essential**

Inside the first-aid kit, you should affix the phone numbers of your veterinarian (both daytime and after-hours numbers), the nearest emergency veterinary hospital, and the local poison control center's number. Keep these taped inside the kit so they will not get lost.

You can assemble a first-aid kit from easily purchasable items:

- Assorted sizes of nonstick bandages, sterile gauze wrappings, pressure bandages, bandage tape, self-adhesive wrap (VetWrap), and bandage scissors
- Disposable latex gloves or rubber gloves
- Triple antibiotic ointment
- Surgical glue or VetBond (available through veterinary supply catalogues)
- Cortisone cream
- Quick muzzle
- Digital thermometer
- Unflavored pediatric electrolyte (Pedialyte), syrup of ipecac, kaolin product (Kaopectate), bismuth subsalicylate (Pepto-Bismol), Benadryl tablets or capsules, and aspirin
- Betadine solution
- Petroleum jelly (Vaseline)
- Mineral oil or activated charcoal
- Hydrogen peroxide
- Tweezers

Important Phone Numbers

Besides a first-aid kit, you should have several phone numbers taped to your phone or nearby in case of an emergency. These include your vet's phone number, an emergency veterinary hospital number, an alternate emergency veterinary hospital number, and a local or national poison control number. You should probably have the names and numbers of local animal control and shelters in case your rottie is missing.

 **Fact**

> The American Red Cross is known for coming to the aid of humans all the time, but did you know it also has tips on caring for pets in disasters? Visit their Web site at *www.redcross.org*.

Disaster Preparedness

Hurricanes, tornados, forest fires, floods, blizzards, and earthquakes are all common natural disasters within the United States. In recent years, terrorism can be added to the list of potential disasters a pet owner may face. We'll take a look at how you can prepare for these disasters.

Where Will You Stay?

Plan your strategy before disaster strikes. Plan where you will stay if something were to happen where you live. The Red Cross does not take pets. If you have family or friends living outside the potential disaster area, talk to them now and make arrangements. Don't assume that they'll be willing to take both you and your rottie. You may find out later that they won't, and you'll be scrambling for other accommodations.

If you don't have family or friends with whom you can stay, make a listing of hotels and motels within a certain radius of your house (five miles, ten miles, twenty-five miles, fifty miles, and so on) that will allow pets. Locate kennels that are outside the potential disaster area in case you must stay in a place that doesn't allow pets. Some hotels will allow pets, but only up to a certain size. Ask before you find yourself in sudden need of their services, and update the list at least once a year.

If you really can't find a place to put your rottie, call around to shelters as a last resort. Most shelters will be full with pets from the disaster, and it is a good place for your rottie to pick up diseases, but if you have no choice, ask the shelter if they will board your rottie.

Emergency Kit

Sometimes you have plenty of warning about an impending natural disaster (hurricanes and floods) and sometimes you have little or no warning (fires, tornados, earthquakes). Be sure to have the following items in an emergency package in a handy place:

- Bowls, leashes, and can opener
- Contact information for hotels, motels, emergency veterinarians, your veterinarian, and other worthwhile numbers
- Copies of your pet's health records and vaccination records
- Enough pet food and potable water for three days
- Pet first-aid kit
- Photos of your pet in case he gets lost
- Travel crates

Worst-Case Scenario

If disaster strikes and you're too far from home, who will rescue your rottie? Find a pet-owning friend or neighbor who lives close to you and whom you can trust. Have an agreement that whoever gets home first will help rescue the other's pet. You'll have to give your neighbor a way to enter your home. Plan in advance a predetermined place to meet so you can pick up your rottie or return her pets to her. Be sure to tell your neighbor about your emergency preparedness package and where it is located so he or she can bring it.

In the event that no one except emergency personnel can get to your house, you can sometimes ask them to rescue your rottweiler. There are emergency stickers you can purchase to put on your windows and alert emergency personnel of animals that need rescuing. Sometimes animal control will come by and rescue pets and take them to the local animal shelter.

 **Alert!**

Don't wait for the authorities to evacuate you. In many cases of formal evacuation, families have little to no time to get out. Keep informed about the emergency situation as it evolves.

How to Muzzle Your Rottie

No matter how gentle your rottie is when he is healthy, he can become a totally different animal when injured and in pain. Dogs frequently bite or snap when in pain and sometimes don't recognize their owner. It is imperative that you muzzle your rottweiler securely before attempting any life-saving procedures or you run the risk of getting bitten. Some conditions require you not to muzzle your dog. In these cases, you may still get a bite, but this is a risk you run with dog ownership. You will have to determine beforehand what risks you are willing to take to try to save your rottweiler's life.

If you do not have a muzzle, you can fashion one from a long strip of bandage, a tie, or cord. (Do not muzzle a dog that is having difficulty breathing.) Start in the middle at the bottom of the dog's muzzle. Wrap the bandage upward, tie, and then bring it back down under the chin and tie. Take the two loose ends and tie them behind the dog's head securely.

Mouth-to-Mouth Resuscitation

Mouth-to-mouth resuscitation can be risky with a big dog such as a rottweiler. Never perform mouth-to-mouth resuscitation on a conscious dog. The dog should not be breathing if you're going to perform mouth-to-mouth.

If your rottie has gotten in trouble in the water and is not breathing, point his head downhill so that the water can run out of his lungs. Press on his rib cage to force the water out. Then, begin mouth-to-mouth. Close your rottweiler's jaws and hold them together. Cup your hand around his jaws to make a funnel between your mouth and his nose. Blow air in and keep an eye on his rib cage. It should expand normally as if he is taking a breath. (Don't overinflate the lungs or you can do damage.) Release, and let the air be expelled. Repeat this several times until your rottie is breathing on his own.

 Essential

If your rottie has suspected internal injuries or broken bones, the safest way to transport him is on a stiff piece of plywood that won't further injure him. If he is wounded or sick, but doesn't have injuries that will be disturbed if he moves around, putting him in a crate will be safer and might keep him from panicking.

Emergencies

With all emergencies, it is best to seek veterinary assistance. You are not a professional and while your intentions are good, you can actually aggravate the situation. Any veterinarian should be able to help your rottie, so if you can take him to the closest veterinarian, you can at least get rudimentary care and triage.

In any emergency situation, you must remain calm so you can make good decisions. Your rottie is counting on you. Don't be afraid to ask for help. While a stranger might not be able to provide you with actual medical care, you may be able to have that person contact the veterinarian on a cell phone and describe the situation.

Animal Bites

Dog bites can cause severe puncture wounds. Many puncture wounds take a few minutes to appear, so check your rottweiler over several times if he was in a dog fight and appears uninjured. If the wounds are not serious, wash them out with a mild mixture of 10 percent betadine and 90 percent water. Your veterinarian will want to see your rottweiler and prescribe antibiotics to reduce the risk of abscesses. Check with the owner of the dog that bit your rottweiler to make sure his rabies vaccinations are current.

If the bite was made by a wild animal that your rottie has killed, do not dispose of the animal. Instead have the local health department check it for rabies. Rabies is still a dangerous disease. Avoid contact with any of the wild animal's fluids (such as blood or saliva). Use latex gloves when handling the dead animal. Your vet may wish to boost your rottie's current vaccinations.

Broken Bones

Fractures to the head, chest, or back may be life-threatening. Keep your rottweiler quiet. While trying to keep him stationary, move him onto a flat board where he can remain rigid. Transport him to a veterinarian immediately.

If your rottweiler has broken his leg, you can fashion a splint from a stick, a rolled-up piece of stiff cardboard, or even a rolled-up newspaper. Place the splint alongside the broken leg and wrap either tape or self-adhesive bandages (such as VetWrap) around it.

Choking

Signs of choking and breathing difficulty include gagging, coughing, wheezing, and gums and tongue turning pale or blue. Do not muzzle the dog, and seek immediate veterinary attention. Loosen your dog's collar and anything else that might restrict breathing. Check your rottweiler's throat for any object that may be caught and obstructing the flow of air. If you see something that you can remove with tweezers, do so. Do not use your fingers, as you can accidentally push the item farther down. If the item is lodged in the throat, try pushing on the dog's abdomen to expel the object. If dog is not breathing, give him mouth-to-mouth resuscitation.

 **Fact**

A severe burn, where the skin is charred or where underlying tissue is exposed, requires immediate veterinary attention. You can treat minor burns over a small area with ice packs or cold water. Do not use water on extensive burns or you may risk shock. Aloe vera is a good burn treatment after the burn blisters.

Deep Cuts or Lacerations

Severe cuts and lacerations will most likely require suturing. Use pressure bandages to slow or stop the bleeding, except in severe crushing injuries. If injuries are severe, such as from a car accident, there may be internal bleeding. Use a stiff board to transport your dog and seek veterinary attention.

Electrocution

If your rottweiler is still touching the electricity source, do not touch him or you may be electrocuted also. Use a wooden broom handle or other nonconductive item to unplug the cord. Treat as you would for shock. Administer mouth-to-mouth resuscitation by closing the dog's mouth and breathing into his nose if he is not breathing. Seek immediate veterinary attention.

Fishhooks

If your dog has stepped on a fishhook or had one pierce his lip, take him to a vet. If no vet is available, you may have to muzzle your rottie and find the barb of the hook. Push the barb through the skin if necessary to expose it, and snip it off with a pair of wire cutters. Then remove the hook. Contact your vet, as he or she may wish to prescribe antibiotics. Only your veterinarian should remove swallowed fishhooks.

Heat Stroke

Signs of dehydration and heat stroke are elevated temperature, extreme thirst, watery diarrhea, vomiting, lethargy, high temperature (over 103°F), skin around muzzle or neck that does not snap back when pinched, difficulty breathing, weakness, and pale gums. Keep in mind that dehydration can occur during any season, not just in the summer.

 **Essential**

Most people know not to leave their dog in a car during the summer, but other places can be just as dangerous. Tents and campers can become very hot. Even standing outdoors without cover can cause heat stroke since rotties are less tolerant of the heat because of their black coats. Heat stroke can occur anywhere there is not enough airflow and it is warm.

In case of heat stroke, do not muzzle your rottie. Move him into the shade or a cool and well-ventilated area. Give him cool water or an unflavored pediatric electrolyte to drink. Soak him in tepid or cool water. Do not use ice-cold water, as it will cause the capillaries to contract and not dissipate heat. Make certain he can breathe, and remove constricting collars or other items. Once this is done, obtain immediate veterinary attention.

You can prevent heat stroke by keeping your rottweiler in well-ventilated areas with shade in the summertime. Always provide fresh water, and do not exercise your rottie when it's hot outside.

Never leave a dog in a car during warm weather, even with the windows down.

Hypothermia and Frostbite

Signs of hypothermia include lowered body temperature, shivering, and lethargy, followed by stupor, shock, unconsciousness, and finally death. Lack of food for energy and dehydration can greatly affect your dog's ability to keep warm. Dogs expend energy and heat while they are working and exercising, but if the heat loss is too great, your dog may experience hypothermia.

Treatment for hypothermia is mostly common sense. Warm your dog slowly by wrapping him in blankets or lying next to him in blankets to help warm him. If he is conscious, you should offer him warm broth to drink. And, of course, seek immediate veterinary attention.

 **Fact**

Your rottie is more likely to suffer from heat exhaustion than hypothermia, but it can still happen. A fall in an icy creek or being left outside without shelter in the winter can bring on hypothermia.

Frostbite is skin damage due to cold. The skin will turn white if frostbitten. If severely frostbitten, the skin will turn black. Sometimes the affected skin will slough off, leaving a raw sore. If the skin is white and intact, warm it slowly in tepid water (not hot—you can damage the skin further). It will be painful to warm the skin. In a case of frostbite where there are sores, wrap with an antibiotic ointment and gauze. In all cases of frostbite, seek veterinary attention.

Insect Bites and Stings

You can treat most insect bites and stings with an over-the-counter antihistamine that your veterinarian can recommend. If your rottweiler shows any allergic reactions to bites or stings (such as severe swelling or difficulty breathing), seek immediate veterinary attention. This can be a life-threatening condition known as an ana-phylactic reaction.

Spider bites can be very serious. The two most dangerous spi-ders are the black widow and the brown recluse. Both of these spider bites can be fatal if left untreated. If you suspect a spider has bitten your rottweiler, seek veterinary attention.

Poisoning

If you suspect your dog has ingested a poison, call your veteri-narian and poison control center immediately for the correct course of action. Have the chemical or substance handy so you can prop-erly describe it to the veterinarian or poison-control center worker. Do not induce vomiting unless told to do so. Some acids, alkalis, and other substances can harm your rottweiler more if aspirated.

Snakebite

Snakebites usually come from pit vipers in the United States: cottonmouths, copperheads, water moccasins, and rattlesnakes. In some warm areas, coral snakes can be a problem. In all cases, keep your rottie quiet to avoid spread of the poison and seek immediate veterinary assistance. Allow the wound to bleed for thirty seconds to draw the poison away. Then clean and disinfect the wound with betadine and apply an elastic tourniquet between the wound and the blood supply if on an extremity. (Do not tie the tourniquet tight; you don't want to cut off circulation.) Then, if you have a snake-bite kit, you will need to use the plunger to draw the venom out. Never suck the wound, or you may become sick on the venom. (t)

CHAPTER 12

Congenital and Hereditary Diseases

THE ROTTWEILER HAS BEEN a very popular breed of dog. For several years, the rottweiler was in the top ten of AKC dog breeds. Now, the rottie's popularity is sagging, but not before the backyard breeders and puppy mill products have taken their toll on the breed. The rottie has many congenital and hereditary problems, which is why when you purchase a rottie you must buy from a responsible breeder. All dogs carry the potential for genetic diseases even though they are healthy. Recessive genes are responsible for a number of hereditary diseases. Because more than one gene may be responsible for a condition, some genetic diseases are difficult to track. OFA, PennHIP, and other organizations are working toward diagnosing genetic diseases with special tests and tracking them through a database.

Bloat

Gastric torsion or canine gastric dilatation-volvulus (CGDV), commonly known as "bloat," is a life-threatening condition that affects deep-chested breeds such as the rottweiler. Nearly 60,000 dogs suffer from bloat each year and of those, one third will die. Rottweilers are at risk for bloat due to their overall conformation.

No one really knows what causes bloat exactly, but there are certain patterns that have been recognized. Older male dogs with deep chests tend to suffer from bloat more than young dogs, female dogs, or dogs with narrow chests, but bloat can occur anytime with any dog. Some suggest that rapid eating, digestive problems, or gulping too much air could be causes. The problem is that there are a number of contributing factors, so no one can point to any single cause.

Dogs that suffer from gastric dilatation experience a rapid onset of gas in the stomach. The gas puts pressure on the internal organs, damaging them in the process. If gastric dilatation becomes severe, the stomach may twist along the axis or torsion, becoming gastric torsion or volvulus. The dog goes into shock and will die a painful death if untreated.

 Fact

If the stomach has not torsioned yet, sometimes giving an antigas medication like simethecone (Gas-X) will help slow down the torsion. Regardless of what medication you give your dog, you must take him to the vet immediately.

How to Recognize Bloat

Bloat is characterized by a distended abdomen, attempted vomiting and retching, salivating, and restlessness. Bloat is a serious life-threatening condition. Obtain emergency veterinary care immediately! Do not attempt to treat this yourself.

If the stomach has twisted, surgery is the only thing that can save your dog. Your veterinarian may have to untwist the stomach and perform a gastroplexy to affix the stomach to the right abdominal wall to prevent further torsion.

Dogs That Are at Risk

Dogs with deep, narrow chests that gulp air along with their food are most at risk. Older dogs are more at risk than younger dogs. Purebred dogs are three times more likely to experience bloat than mixed breeds. Feeding large meals and exercising a dog after it has eaten may increase the risk of bloat. There also may be hereditary and environmental factors.

Preventing Bloat

To help prevent bloat, feed your dog several smaller meals over the day rather than one large one. Watch your rottweiler after he eats. Bloat usually occurs within three hours after mealtimes. Adding water to dry food aids in its evacuation from the stomach. Dog food soaked in water will evacuate from the stomach in about twenty to forty minutes, whereas dry dog food alone can take up to two and a half hours or longer to leave the stomach. Also, don't change dog food drastically. Sudden changes in diet can cause digestive problems.

 **Essential**

If there is no time, you can possibly relieve the gas pressure that comes from bloat by using a plastic surgical tube. Ask your vet how to perform this procedure before you try it. You can seriously injure your rottweiler if you don't know how to perform it properly.

Cataracts

Cataracts or cloudiness of the eye's lens can be due to either hereditary or environmental reasons. Juvenile cataracts are usually hereditary. It may appear as a dot or may cloud the entire lens. A veterinary ophthalmologist can determine if your rottie has cataracts. Sometimes surgery to remove the cloudy lens will help restore sight. It is very important that your rottie's parents have their eyes certified through CERF.

Hip Dysplasia

Hip dysplasia (HD) is a crippling hereditary disease in which the dog's hips are malformed. Therefore it is very important for your rottweiler's parents to be OFA-certified with a hip rating of good or excellent. Your breeder may choose to get certification through PennHIP.

Hip Dysplasia in Rottweilers

Between the years 1974 and 2002, breeders and owners registered 81,313 rottweilers with the OFA. Out of these dogs, OFA diagnosed 20.7 percent as dysplastic. Since OFA is a voluntary registry, the percentage may be higher due to failure of reporting dysplastic dogs. Clearly, hip dysplasia is common enough in rottweilers to warrant caution when selecting a dog or puppy.

 Fact

Hip dysplasia is prevalent in all purebreds and in mixed breed dogs. It can be very mild to severe. There is no way of telling that a dog has hip dysplasia except through x-rays. Corrective surgery is very expensive. In many cases, it costs several thousands of dollars.

Nutrition and Hip Dysplasia

No amount of good nutrition can prevent hip dysplasia. There are nutritional supplements that will mitigate the effects, but food cannot cure the disease. You can, however, *cause* environmentally induced hip dysplasia by subjecting a puppy or young dog to extreme physical stress or poor nutrition.

Options in Hip Dysplasia

In mildly dysplastic cases, your veterinarian may be able to mitigate it with anti-inflammatories such as Rimadyl, Metacam,

Dermamax, or Zubrin, or nutritional aids such as glucosamine, chondroitin, and creatine. Serious cases may require expensive surgery. Some extreme cases of hip dysplasia may be so painful that the humane thing to do is to euthanize the dog.

Elbow Dysplasia and Osteochondrosis Dissecans

Elbow dysplasia (ED) and osteochondrosis dissecans (OCD) are very much alike and can be related. In fact, if OCD occurs along with ED, the OCD is considered hereditary.

Elbow Dysplasia

Elbow dysplasia is a hereditary disease in which the dog's elbow joints are malformed. Like hip dysplasia, no amount of nutrition or supplements can prevent it. Dogs with elbow dysplasia may walk or stand "out at the elbows." All dogs with elbow dysplasia have osteoarthritis. It is very important to make sure your rottweiler's parents are OFA-certified and cleared of elbow dysplasia.

 Fact

Between 1974 and 2002, breeders and owners registered 7,293 rottweilers with the OFA for elbow dysplasia. Out of these dogs, OFA diagnosed a staggering 41.8 percent as dysplastic, making this the second worst breed for elbow dysplasia (second only to chows).

The elbow dysplasia certification is not as common as the hip dysplasia, possibly because breeders may be unaware of the need to certify their dogs. What's more, the OFA registry is entirely voluntary, meaning that breeders and owners do not have to register a dysplastic dog.

Osteochondrosis Dissecans

OCD is a condition in which the cartilage thickens in joint areas. This thickened cartilage is more prone to damage and may tear and form a flap or rejoin to the bone. OCD may appear in several joints or only one. If your rottweiler has this condition, he may develop a limp after exercising, suggesting that perhaps he has sustained an injury. However, OCD will cause persistent lameness. You may feel the joint pop or crackle as you examine it. Its onset is usually between four and eight months of age.

If your rottie is diagnosed with OCD, your veterinarian may recommend that you rest your dog for several weeks. Some dogs require surgery to remove the lesions or any loose cartilage. OCD may be hereditary, so dogs with this disease should not be bred.

Entropion and Ectropion

Both entropion and ectropion are conditions of the eyelid. They're exceedingly uncomfortable and often require surgery to correct them. Both are also disqualifying faults in the show ring.

Entropion is a hereditary condition in which the eyelid turns inward into the eye, causing the eyelashes and fur to rub against the eyeball. It is obviously irritating to the dog and usually requires surgery to correct it.

Ectropion shows itself in drooping of the lower eyelid, exposing its interior. In mild cases, your veterinarian may prescribe eye drops and antibiotic and corticosteroid ophthalmic ointment. In severe cases, surgery may be required.

Epilepsy

Epilepsy is a condition that exists in all kinds of dogs, whether purebred or mixed breed. It is usually hereditary in dogs and is quite prevalent in some lines. Idiopathic epilepsy in dogs is very similar to epilepsy in humans. However, with some forms of epilepsy, environmental causes must be ruled out before the condition can be declared idiopathic epilepsy. These causes include trauma to the head, poisoning, tick paralysis, parasites, certain vitamin deficiencies, overheating, intestinal obstructions, liver problems, and calcium imbalances.

 Essential

There's a type of epilepsy that's known as rage syndrome, or "Springer Rage Syndrome" because of the prevalence in springer spaniels. Rage syndrome causes the dog to attack for no apparent reason and then become "normal" again without realizing he's attacked or done damage. These seizures are incurable. The dog must be put down or risk severe injury or even death.

Seizures come in two types: petit mal and grand mal. Petit mal seizures tend to look like a space-out, a nervous twitch, or clumsiness; the dog may fall over, snarl, or blank out. Grand mal seizures are full-blown seizures that cause shaking or convulsions. The dog may make strange noises or cry out and may urinate or empty his bowels.

If your rottweiler is epileptic, your vet will need to perform some tests to rule out other causes. If the seizures are frequent or become worse, usually your vet will prescribe a medication to help control the seizures. You should never breed a dog with epilepsy because of the potential hereditary component.

Hypothyroidism

Hypothyroidism is when the dog's thyroid produces insufficient thyroid hormones. Symptoms can include lethargy, dull and dry coat, obesity or weight gain, and a thinning coat. The dog may seek warmer areas. Hypothyroidism can cause infertility in intact males and females.

Some forms of hypothyroidism may be hereditary, so it is inadvisable to breed a hypothyroid dog. Your veterinarian can diagnose hypothyroidism through a blood test. If your rottweiler is hypothyroid, your veterinarian may prescribe a form of thyroid hormone.

 **fact**

OFA has a thyroid registry that is relatively new. As of December 2002, only 195 dogs had been registered with this OFA registry, and of those, only 73.8 percent of those dogs are normal. Breeders should test and register their rottweilers with the OFA.

Paneosteitis

Paneosteitis, or pano, is a condition in which a growing puppy suddenly becomes lame. This lameness may be mild to severe and may affect different parts of the puppy at different times. The onset of pano is somewhere around five to twelve months of age and usually affects males more than females. Large and giant breeds such as the rottweiler are more often affected by pano. It may or may not have a genetic component.

If your puppy has pano, your veterinarian may prescribe analgesics and rest. He may ask you to limit exercise. Eventually, as the puppy gets older, the pain subsides and the puppy grows out of it.

Pano is painful, but in the long term this disease is not detrimental to your rottie's health. Some breeders believe that pano is caused when the dog grows too fast in some places for other parts of him to catch up, causing pain. Since this is not a permanent condition, it does not affect the dog once he is fully grown. Most rottie owners are glad to know that their pups will outgrow their "growing pains."

Retinal Atrophy

Progressive retinal atrophy (PRA) and central progressive retinal atrophy (CPRA) are two degenerative eye disorders that lead to blindness. A veterinary ophthalmologist can determine whether your rottweiler has these or other eye diseases. CERF provides a registry for dogs intended for breeding. The CERF evaluation lasts for one year. Any rottweiler that you buy should have parents that are both registered with CERF. If you plan to breed your rottweiler, you will need to have its eyes examined and have it registered with CERF as well.

 **Fact**

Eye diseases that can lead to blindness include glaucoma, juvenile cataracts, and progressive retinal atrophy. It is very hard to screen for these diseases in breeding dogs because they may appear without warning later in the dog's life. This is why CERF certification only lasts one year.

Subaortic Stenosis

Subaortic stenosis (SAS) is an insidious hereditary condition that may show no outward sign in an apparently healthy dog. Suddenly, the dog may simply drop over, dead. A narrowing of the outflow tract of the left ventricle is what causes SAS. In this case, the narrowing occurs below the aortic valve. The heart must work harder to push more blood through the narrow opening, causing more problems.

 **Alert!**

Signs of heart problems vary. Your rottie may tire easier or have trouble breathing, running, or being active. In severe cases, his skin may turn pale or blue, or he may have fluid buildup in his legs. He may faint. Any of these symptoms are serious, and you should have your rottweiler examined by a vet.

SAS can be difficult to diagnose. The heart murmur, a common symptom of SAS, may be difficult to detect. The dog may also have arrhythmias. A veterinary cardiologist can diagnose SAS through either Doppler echocardiography or cardiac catheterization. The prognosis for a long, healthy life is poor.

Dogs with SAS should not be bred since this is a genetic disease that may be passed to future generations. OFA has a cardiac registry, but there are very few dogs registered with the registry (only 1,192 dogs as of December). Only purchase a puppy from a reputable breeder who has cleared dogs registered with the OFA.

Von Willebrand's Disease

Von Willebrand's disease (VWD) is a type of hemophilia in dogs. There are various levels of hemophilia, and some dogs suffer from a more severe form than others. There are two types of VWD: inherited and acquired. The acquired form of VWD is in association with familial autoimmune thyroid disease. Your veterinarian can diagnose VWD through a blood test. Only dogs cleared of VWD should be bred.

Dogs with VWD are more susceptible to uncontrolled bleeding. If your rottie has VWD, your veterinarian should take precautions during surgery to avoid having the dog bleed out. Likewise, you should take precautions to lessen the chances that your rottweiler might become injured.

Chapter 13

Choosing a Trainer

WHEN IT COMES TO TRAINING your rottweiler, should you go it alone, or is it better to work with a professional dog trainer? There are pros and cons to training your dog yourself, while there are usually benefits to taking your rottie to a professional trainer. But not all trainers are the same, and not all will be right for your rottweiler. This chapter discusses whether you should train your rottweiler by yourself or hire a professional trainer. It also discusses trainers and types of training classes available.

Training Your Rottie Yourself

You may be wondering if you should train your rottweiler or if you should sign up for training classes. Training a dog isn't rocket science, but it still requires experience and talent. Oddly enough, people expect themselves to be experts when it comes to dog training—and these are the same people who would normally have someone teach their children or pay a professional to repair something in their home. So why is it that people expect to be dog experts and able to train a dog by themselves or with a book?

As mentioned earlier, dog training isn't rocket science. But training your dog without a professional to help you is a little like learning brain surgery through correspondence courses—yes, you'll get the fundamentals, but you may not like the results. If you've successfully trained dogs before, you shouldn't have much trouble training your rottie. But even so, you may want to learn newer training techniques.

 **Alert!**

Be cautious of using outdated training methods such as the "alpha roll" or "jerking the collar." While these indeed do have a place in training, it is a very small one and should not be used constantly. Harsh methods can elicit aggressive responses, something you don't want to do with your rottie.

Using This Book for Training

If you've never trained a dog before and want to "go it alone," the information in this book will help you. The training discussed here is primarily positive reinforcement—that is, rewarding a dog for doing the right thing. In positive reinforcement, there is less chance of causing aggressive behavior due to harsh punishment.

However, there is plenty of room for mistakes even with this approach, as one training method doesn't fit all dogs. An experienced trainer has many methods in his or her repertoire, and if one doesn't work with a dog, he or she can choose another. Teaching your rottie the right way the first time is much better than trying to fix a problem that develops later. It is always easier to teach the correct behavior than it is to correct a problem.

Time and Training a Dog

Time is another consideration. If you're a novice at dog training, you can expect that it will take longer training your dog on your own than if you attended a training class. If you're still convinced that you should train your rottie by yourself, use this book and look for other recent books on dog training that stress positive reinforcement methods. You can later decide to take your rottie to a professional trainer, if it is not working out.

Training Methods

You'll hear a lot about positive reinforcement training when you study current methods. In positive reinforcement, you reward good behavior and ignore bad behavior, hoping to shape your dog's behavior toward the good behavior side. In some training methods, the word "no" and correction are never used. When you use positive reinforcement, you give your rottie praise, a toy, or a treat when he performs a desired action. For example, you tell your rottie to sit and he sits. You give him a treat. When you start training, you'll want to use these positive methods. You'll enjoy it, and your rottie will enjoy it, too.

 Essential

Hitting, kicking, slapping, and yelling at your rottie are all forms of abuse. Don't abuse your rottie—ever. These forms of punishment aren't meaningful to a dog. They only serve to make him fearful and aggressive toward you.

This book describes primarily positive methods, but it does recommend correction when correction is necessary. When correcting a dog, you use the least amount of correction necessary to achieve the desired result. The correction must be meaningful to the action, and the correction must occur during or shortly after the action you wish to correct.

Correction can be a single word, such as "No!", or it can be the harsh sound of a metal can of pennies being shaken, or it can mean that your rottie has to sit when he's jumping around. All of these actions are a form of correction.

You want to be someone your rottie can respect, not fear. Most rottweilers are very attached to their favorite person. When you behave badly, you damage his perception of you. Be the person your rottie thinks you are.

Looking for the Right Trainer

If you're one of those people who has decided not to go it alone to train your rottie, good for you! You can't know everything. Now you must decide on an appropriate trainer for your rottie.

You can ask your rottie's breeder and veterinarian if they have any trainer recommendations. If you have friends with well-trained dogs, you can ask them whom they would recommend. Often people who compete in agility, obedience, or tracking can point you toward good trainers. If you can't get a recommendation, you may have to look in the yellow pages under "Dog Trainers" and check some out on your own.

 Fact

Go to an obedience or agility trial. Quite often, top trainers in the region will be at these trials competing with their dogs. If you see someone competing with a rottweiler, you can ask her whom she goes to for training or if she has any recommendations.

Training Facilities

There are various training facilities available. Some are cheap, and some are expensive. The cheaper ones are usually available at community colleges, pet-supply stores, and other discount places. As a rule, you get what you pay for. Many of these trainers are novices or only train according to the methods required by the stores. While these may be fine for generic training, if you're having issues with your rottie, you may not get the training you need. Likewise, they aren't going to prepare your rottie and you for competition.

Don't send your rottweiler away to boarding school! The best trainers train you to train your dog. These trainers understand that you, not them, need to have command over your dog. When you send your rottie away for training, he learns to respect the trainer, not you.

What to Look for in a Trainer

When you look for a training class, look for the following in the trainer:

- Uses positive techniques or mostly positive techniques
- Aims to train you to train your dog
- Has titles on her own dogs
- Has successfully trained rottweilers before
- Will allow you to watch a class
- Happy to provide references
- Offers advanced classes, such as competitive obedience and agility

Visiting a Training Facility

When you visit a training facility, look around. Trainers love to show off their successes. Are there photos of dogs the trainer has handled? Are there mirrors on the walls so the students can see themselves and their dogs? Are the floors protected with nonskid mats so that there's less of a chance of slipping and falling? Is there room for training, or are the dogs cramped? Some training classes are held in places not conducive to training. Pet-supply stores, for example, can be noisy and intimidating. At the same time, they provide good distraction work.

The trainer should be happy to allow you to sit in one of her training classes. If she hedges, you should probably look elsewhere, as there are no "secrets" in dog training. Watch how the trainer interacts with the dogs and owners in her class. The trainer should have a good command of the class and be clear in her directions. Is she teaching the owners how to handle their dogs properly? Are the recommendations good?

Lastly, do you *like* the trainer? Does she make sense to you? Does she genuinely like dogs? Is she harsh or kind with them? Again, look for a training facility that mostly uses positive reinforcement. Harsh techniques may be needed for Schutzhund work (for bite training, for example) but should seldom be needed for obedience.

 **Essential**

Ask the trainer if she would show her dog to you if she has her own pet there. Ask what titles her dog has. Most trainers love to show off their dogs and the titles their dogs have. You can get an idea how the trainer will act with your dog by watching her interact with her dog.

Be aware that not all dog trainers use the same training methods. Some trainers use older, coercive methods that are harsh and outdated. Other trainers use strictly positive methods with no correction at all. Some discount trainers are only trained in a particular style or are unable to handle serious behavioral issues. You want a trainer who uses mostly positive methods but who is knowledgeable in all methods of dog training.

Just as one size doesn't fit all, one training method may or may not work for your rottie. The best way to train is to use as many positive methods as possible, but realize there may be a point when other training methods may be required.

Training Classes Available

Most trainers offer a variety of training classes, depending on the level of dog. For example, if your rottie is a puppy younger than six months, he should probably first attend a puppy kindergarten or KPT session. The following is a short list of what a trainer might offer at her facility:

- **Puppy kindergarten:** Socialization and training for young puppies
- **Beginning obedience:** Training for older puppies and adult dogs

- **Novice obedience:** Training for novice-level competition
- **Open obedience:** Training for open-level competition
- **Utility obedience:** Training for utility competition
- **Conformation:** Training for dog shows or the conformation ring
- **Agility (beginners and advanced):** Training for the sport of agility, in which the dog must traverse an obstacle course in a set amount of time
- **Tracking:** Training for tracking titles, which require the dog to follow a path and look for certain "articles"
- **Herding:** Training to actually herd sheep, ducks, or cattle
- **Flyball:** Training for the fast-paced, timed sport of flyball, in which the dog jumps over several hurdles, hits the flyball box, catches a tennis ball as it flies through the air, and returns over the hurdles
- **Clicker training:** Training method using clickers to reinforce the behavior you want
- **Attention:** Training method in which you teach the dog to focus on you
- **Canine Good Citizen:** training class to prepare your dog for his CGC certificate

 **Question?**

What is clicker training?

Clicker training is a type of positive reinforcement training in which the dog associates the click of the clicker with a treat you give him afterward. The click is a more definite reinforcement than saying "Good dog!" at the time of the action you want to reinforce.

When you start training your rottie, you'll want to sign up for either puppy kindergarten or basic obedience. Training classes are usually one hour a week for six to twelve weeks, depending on the class. They're held at the same time each week and usually have anywhere from three to twelve in a class. Let's look at some of the classes.

Puppy Kindergarten

Puppy kindergarten is a great way to socialize your rottie puppy. It helps socialize him to situations you may not normally be able to expose him to. Your puppy gets to interact with other puppies and their owners so that it helps socialize him and makes him well adjusted. You may also teach your puppy to respond to clickers (a positive reinforcement training device) and may even teach him a few simple commands such as "Sit" and "Down." Puppy kindergarten is usually for puppies younger than six months.

Beginning Obedience

Beginning obedience teaches most of the basic commands: "Sit," "Down," "Come," "Heel," "Stay," and "Stand." This class is usually used as a precursor to novice obedience classes.

Beginning obedience either leads up to novice training or may work toward training your dog to be a good pet. Some beginning obedience classes work toward a Canine Good Citizen certificate, but most work on the fundamentals of obedience training and general house manners. These classes are usually for dogs older than six months.

Novice

Novice obedience is the first step in competitive obedience. Your rottie can earn his Companion Dog (CD) title when he competes in the novice ring. Novice class is for those who wish to compete in the AKC novice obedience trials and earn their Companion Dog certificate.

This class is structured toward training your dog in the fundamentals of the novice ring and practicing just as though you were competing in the novice class. It includes heeling on leash in a pattern, heeling in a figure eight, stand/stay for examination by the judge, sit, down, recall and finish, heeling off-leash in a pattern, long sit/stay (one minute), and long down/stay (three minutes).

 **Alert!**

Be wary of the trainer who has no titles on her dog. How can she possibly teach you in competitive training if she's never finished a dog in a competitive sport?

The Canine Good Citizen

The Canine Good Citizen test is offered through the AKC. Any dog, purebred or mixed breed, can compete for a CGC title. The test is pass or fail. The dog must pass all ten tests to qualify for the CGC title. The good news is that if your rottie fails the CGC, he can retake it at any time without penalties. These tests include accepting a friendly stranger, sitting politely for petting, appearance and grooming, walking on a loose lead, walking through a crowd, sit and down on command, staying in place, coming when called, reaction to another dog, reaction to distraction, and supervised separation.

Checklist for Finding a Trainer

It is okay to ask lots of questions when looking for a trainer. In fact, most trainers expect to hear questions and are glad to answer them. The following is a checklist of questions you should ask a trainer before signing your dog up for classes.

- ❑ How many years have you been training dogs?
- ❑ What titles have you put on dogs?
- ❑ Have you trained rottweilers? What titles have those rottweilers earned?
- ❑ What types of classes do you offer?
- ❑ Do you use positive reinforcement training or some other type of training? How much of it is positive reinforcement?

☐ When do you offer classes? When is the next available class?

☐ Do you hold any certifications?

☐ Have you written any books? Which ones?

☐ Do you offer a written guarantee? If so, what do you guarantee?

☐ After my rottie and I finish the course, are there drop-in classes so that we can practice?

☐ Do you offer any one-on-one training classes?

☐ Do you offer behavioral counseling?

☐ Do you offer any other services (such as grooming, doggie day care)?

☐ Do you have any clients I can contact for recommendations?

☐ How large are your typical classes?

Many of these questions have no right or wrong answers. When you meet with the trainer, you want to be sure that her training style and personality agree with yours. You also need to know if the trainer is comfortable working with rottweilers. Some trainers only like to work with easily trained dogs or certain breeds. If you sense that the trainer may not like to train rottweilers, look for another trainer.

Regardless of the trainer you choose, realize that if something isn't working out for you right now, you can look for a better trainer elsewhere. Once you find an excellent trainer, you'll be glad you did—and so will your rottie! 🐾

CHAPTER 14

Basic Obedience

EVERY DOG NEEDS TO KNOW basic obedience commands and the rottweiler is no exception. Basic obedience can make the difference between a pleasurable pet and a nuisance. Rottweilers are big, powerful dogs, and if you don't have control over them, they can be intimidating.

Simple Obedience

So, what commands should your rottie know? And how hard are they to teach? Every dog should know how to walk on a leash without pulling, sit, down, stay, come, and heel. These are the basics when it comes to teaching your rottie good manners.

These commands aren't particularly difficult to teach. Most rotties are very smart and can learn a command after a few repetitions. But it takes practice to have a dog that is reliable in obeying commands. You may have taught your rottie to sit on command, but only with practice will you teach him to sit *every time* on command. You'll have to practice with your rottie every day to have a reliable dog.

Luckily, practicing commands only takes a few minutes from your day. You and your rottie can even practice them while you do other things. For example, you can work on sit/stays and down/stays while you're watching television. When you're walking your rottie, you can work on "Heel," "Walk nicely on leash,"

"Come," and "Sit." You can practice commands anywhere. Think about what you do during the day and how you can slip in a few commands during the moments you're with your rottie. You can enforce a down/stay before you feed him, or give him the "Come" command when you call him from the yard or from another room.

Essential

Five to ten minutes of training every day will reinforce the lessons while making the session fun and practical for you. Keep them short, and end on a positive note.

Before you start training, you must have the proper tools for the job. Have you ever tried to use a flat screwdriver or a penny to loosen a Phillips-head screw? Tough, isn't it? The same is true with collars and leashes. Using the wrong collar or leash during training could be troublesome. Let's look at what you should use when you train your rottie.

Training Collars

Training collars have been a controversial subject in recent years as positive methods have become more popular. Many positive trainers abhor slip collars and prong collars, which many call "choke collars" and "pinch collars." They prefer flat (buckle) collars and head harnesses to control their dogs. The truth is that the training collar is a tool, and like any tool, it can be misused. If you use these collars correctly, they are very humane, and your rottie will learn commands easily. However, there is a potential for abuse. If you are determined not to abuse your rottie, you can use these without inflicting pain or punishment. Let's look at the collars and investigate their proper applications.

 **fact**

Fitting your rottweiler's training collar is very important. In the case of slip, semi-slip, snap chokes, and prong collars, the collar should fit snugly high around the neck without any left-over collar hanging down.

Flat Collars and Slip Collars

Your rottie should wear a flat collar (buckle) at all times and should have identification tags attached to it. Slip collars have been called "choke chains" in the past, but of course you should never use them to choke your rottie. They are made of nylon, rope, or chain with a ring at either end. The chain or rope slips through the opposite ring to form a collar. Your rottie should only wear his slip collar during training or while you're present. A limited slip collar tightens, but it has a catch that only lets it tighten to a certain point, thus making it difficult to choke a dog.

 **Essential**

There's a right way and a wrong way to put on a slip collar. When you get ready to put the slip collar on your rottie, have him sit facing you. Hold the collar up and look at it. It should look like the letter "P" when it is going over his head. If it looks like a backward "P," you are putting it on backward.

Snap chokes are slip collars that are made of parachute cord. Instead of two fixed rings at each end, they have a ring and a snap device with a loose ring around the parachute cord. When you put the snap choke on your rottie's neck, you affix the snap to the loose ring, thus making it a better fit.

Prong Collars

Prong collars look like medieval torture devices, but they are actually quite humane. They're called pinch collars by some because the prongs pull inward against the dog's skin and hold it. Prong collars work well for dogs with thick necks that tend to pull hard. The collars work with a minimal amount of pressure, providing good control over the dog without choking him or ripping his fur. AKC forbids the use of prong collars on show grounds. You should only use a prong collar under the supervision of a professional trainer. Never leave a prong collar on your rottie unsupervised.

Head Halters

Head halters control the dog's head by applying pressure to his muzzle, which makes it easy to lead him around. Many dogs respond well to head halters, and thus many positive trainers use head halters as a "humane alternative" to other types of training collars. However, head halters too have their problems. If improperly fit, a dog is able to paw one off. Because the head halter wraps around the muzzle, it can restrict breathing. Dogs that fight the head halter can injure their necks and spines. Head halters look like muzzles, and they tend to increase other people's apprehension about your rottweiler. In most dog shows (AKC and others), head halters aren't allowed.

Leashes

Just as there are a variety of collars on the market, there are also several types of leashes. Most people buy the wrong leash, which can be defined as one that provides no control over a big dog like your rottweiler. You should have two or three leashes for different circumstances. The leashes you should definitely have are a leather leash and a tracking leash.

You should purchase a good, sturdy six-foot leather leash. Unlike the cheap nylon imitators, the leather leash is kind on your hands and won't cut into your hands the way nylon and rope leashes will. They give better control than any other leash. Yes, a leather leash is more expensive, but you must use the right tool for the job. Also purchase a good fifteen to twenty-foot tracking leash (nylon or cotton). You can use this for hiking or for training your rottie to come.

Alert!

Never use a training collar for your rottie's everyday collar, and never affix anything (like tags) on the training collar. These collars can get snagged while your dog is unsupervised and choke him.

Leashes you shouldn't use include nylon, rope, chain, and the retractable type. None of these leashes gives you good control over your rottie. One very popular leash is the retractable kind. People love these leashes because their dogs can wander all over without their really having to pay attention to where the dog is going. The problem with these leashes is twofold. They don't offer any control over the dog, even with the line in the lock position. Second, dogs have entangled with other dogs on these leashes and fights have ensued. Unless you have a pocketknife handy to cut the retractable leash cords, there is no way you're going to get your dog out of the fight or the tangle. However, retractable leashes do have their place. They make excellent tools for teaching your dog to come.

Clicker Training

In recent years, both positive reinforcement and clicker training have become popular. This book describes the positive reinforcement techniques involved in teaching commands, but we also investigate an alternative, the clicker training method. These two training methods work well, together or apart, so don't be afraid to try either or both. If your rottie doesn't do well with one, try another approach. Always remember that there is more than one way to train.

Clicker training is fun for both you and your rottweiler. It uses a form of operant conditioning—that is, your rottie receives a reward depending on his actions. It requires that you carry a clicker and a target stick.

How Clicker Training Works

The clicker works because you click whenever your rottie does something you wanted him to do. It is a much more definite sound than saying "Good dog!" when he does something right. When your rottie doesn't do what you want, he doesn't get a click. Now, to make the clicker special, you associate it with food. Every time you click, you follow that click up with a treat. Click, treat; click, treat; click, treat. Your rottie will associate the correct action (the one you clicked for) with the treat. It is a very powerful training method, and you can use it to train your rottie in obedience or to teach him fun tricks.

 **Esseñtial**

To train your rottie to the clicker, have a bunch of small treats available. Usually tiny pieces of hot dogs, cheese, or lunch-meat work well. Dice these into tiny pieces because you'll be feeding a lot.

Introduction to the Clicker

To start clicker training, click the clicker, and then give your rottie a treat. Continue to click and treat until your rottie starts looking at you expectantly when he hears the click. He now associates the click with the food.

Varying the time between the click and treat teaches your rottie to expect the treat sometime after the click. You'll also want to vary where you treat your rottie. For example, you might want to hand him a treat one moment and toss it on the ground the next. Give him different places to find the treat. You can even reinforce the association of food with the clicker by clicking before you set down your rottie's food bowl at feeding time.

Introduction to the Target Stick

The target stick is another clicker tool. Once your rottie is familiar with the clicker, you can use the target stick to teach him to touch things. A target stick is about two to three feet long. Hold it out for your rottie. If he is curious, he'll naturally sniff the stick. When he does, click and treat. At that point, he may become very interested in the stick, so click and treat each time he touches the stick.

◀ Taking time out for a quick pose.

You'll then want him to associate a word with the touch. Say, "Touch!" and as he noses or paws the stick, then click and treat. Try differentiating between the types of touches: nose or paw. Move the stick around and see how he touches it and gradually add the commands "Nose" or "Paw." Click and treat only when he performs the command properly.

Walk Nicely on Leash

It is no fun getting dragged all over the place when you and your rottie are out walking. One of the first things you'll want to work on with your dog is to get him used to the leash.

Positive Method

Start by clipping your rottie's leash to his training collar and let him get used to the pull of the leash. If he gets frantic and tries to pull away, try clipping the leash to his flat collar (just be sure his flat collar is on snugly).

Your rottie may pull a bit on the leash. Give him time to walk around and figure out what he can and can't do on the leash as you hold it. When he's done exploring the limits of the leash, try offering a treat to lure him into a loose leash. Give him the treat when the leash slackens.

 **Essential**

You can usually purchase a clicker and target stick at a pet-supply store; however, if you're having difficulty finding these, you can order them online from groundbreaking clicker trainer Karen Pryor, at *www.clickertraining.com.*

As you start walking, have a treat in your hand and show it to your rottie. Keep his attention focused on you as you walk, occasionally giving him a treat for paying attention to you. As you walk with him, use the treat to keep him from forging ahead or lagging behind. A few sessions will make him easy to walk with.

Clicker Method

Start by clipping a leash on your rottie's collar. Let him walk around and explore what he can and can't do on the leash as you hold it. When he's done exploring the limits of the leash and lets the leash go slack, click and treat. When he tightens on the leash, do nothing. When the leash goes slack, click and treat. He will soon try to keep the leash slack as you hold it.

The next step is to get your dog used to walking in the direction that you want him to go. As he walks in the right direction, click and treat him. Ignore him if he forges ahead or lags behind. Click and treat him only when he is going in the same direction as you and not pulling on the leash.

Sit

Sitting is a simple command. Most dogs learn how to sit easily, but a few may need a little encouragement.

Positive Method

Put your rottie on a loose leash, and hold a treat over his nose. Bring the treat backward while gently pushing on your rottie's rear. Command him to sit using his name. If your rottweiler is stubborn about sitting, try having him sit next to a wall. Once he does sit, give him the treat and praise him. Practice this a few times, and soon your rottie will be sitting on his own.

 Alert!

Don't confuse the commands. Use one-word commands such as "Sit," "Down," and "Come." Don't say, "Fido, sit down!" That's confusing. Use "Sit" for sit and "Down" for lie down. Don't mix commands either. "Down" means to lie down; "Off" means all four paws on the floor.

Clicker Method

The second way to teach your rottie to sit is the preferred way. You wait for the behavior to occur, and then you click and treat. Your rottie will try to duplicate the move to earn the reward. You can then pair the established behavior with the command "Sit."

Another way to teach this command is to put your rottie on a loose leash. Take a treat, or use the target stick and hold it over his nose. Bring the treat or target stick backward. As he follows the treat or the target stick and his rump starts to go down, click and treat. If he just keeps backing up, do this next to a wall so that he must sit. Try again, but this time click and treat as his rump touches the floor. Try this a few more times before adding the command, "Fido, sit!" Use the treat or target stick to move your rottie to the sitting position, following up with a click and treat. Gradually eliminate the target stick or treat, and click and treat only when your rottie sits after the command.

Down

Down is a useful command, especially when you need good control over your rottie. Paired with the "Stay" command, it can be quite useful.

Positive Method

With your rottweiler on a leash, take a treat and lower it from his nose to the ground, close to his chest. Say his name and add the command "Down!" Gently push his shoulders if he doesn't go all the way down. Remember to reward him when he gets it right, and keep practicing!

Clicker Method

Put your rottie on a loose leash and place him in a sit. Take a treat or use the target stick and hold it under his chin. Lower the treat or target stick toward his chest. As he follows the treat or the target stick and his shoulders start to drop, click and treat. Try again, but this time click and treat as his chest touches the floor. Add the command "Fido, down!" while using the treat or target stick. Build up to eliminating the props so your rottweiler goes down on command, and always follow up with a click and treat.

 **Fact**

You can also wait until your dog performs a certain behavior and reward him after it occurs with a click and treat. Again, eventually pairing the click and treat with the command will complete the training.

Come

"Come" is a very important command. You need to be able to call your rottie to you at any time. Enforcing this command early will be beneficial to you and your dog because you'll be better able to prevent your dog from running away or wandering up to strangers.

You should always praise or give your rottie treats for coming to you. Never call your rottweiler over for punishment; otherwise, he'll never come to you when it is important. If you must correct your rottie, go to him. Don't call him to you.

Positive Method

Naturally, you're praising and giving your rottie treats for coming to you. This is a good first step. But you need to make his behavior reliable. Start in an enclosed space, and clip his six-foot leash to his collar. Walk out six feet, turn around, and call your rottie by name, followed by the "Come" command. Use a happy voice, and show him a treat if necessary. If he doesn't come to you, use the leash to bring him toward you. Be positive and happy, and give him the treat.

Now, put him in a sit again, and walk out to the end of his leash. Be careful that he doesn't break his sit in his enthusiasm to come to you. If he does, tell him "No, sit," and put him back in his sit. Don't sound angry when you do this, but instead just be matter-of-fact. Then tell him again to come.

Practice "Come" at short distances. Then gradually lengthen the distance with a long line or retractable leash. When you call your rottweiler, either retract the leash or quickly reel in the long line. If, at any time, your rottie fails to come directly to you, return to shorter distances.

Once you've practiced "Come" for a while at different distances, you need to add distractions. A busy park is a good place to train. Practice "Come" on leash with distractions. If at any time your rottie becomes distracted, shorten the distance and try again. Continue to practice at home in an enclosed area to reinforce the command.

 **Essential**

Always reward your rottweiler for coming to you, whether you call him or not. All good things must come from you. Even if he's done something bad, such as getting loose and running around the neighborhood, always give him a treat for coming back to you.

Eventually, you will want to practice off-leash recalls. When you do practice, find an enclosed area such as your backyard, a dog-training area at a local park, or maybe an enclosed baseball diamond. If your rottie does take off, you should be able to catch him. If such an escape attempt does happen, you need to return to working with him on a short leash. When he is reliable on "Come," you can try him again off leash. Keep practicing even after he comes without any hesitation.

Clicker Method

Use the clicker to click and treat whenever your rottie comes to you. Soon you'll find him coming to you for even the smallest distance. Add the command, "Fido, come!" to get him to come to you on command. Click and treat each time.

Now that your rottie knows how to come, you need to make the behavior reliable. Start in an enclosed space and clip his six-foot leash to his collar. Walk out six feet, turn around, and call your rottie by name followed by the command, using a happy tone of voice. You'll do this just as you would for the positive training method. You can use different settings to test reliability, such as open and enclosed settings, but err on the side of safety if in doubt.

Heel

Heeling is more important for obedience competition than it is for basic obedience, but it is still important to learn. After all, there will be times when you'll want your rottie walking right beside you instead of in front of you, such as when you're walking through a crowd or in a place where you aren't sure of your footing.

 Fact

Heel requires some fancy footwork on your part. When starting out in heel position, lead with your left foot. When you want your rottweiler to stay, lead with your right foot. These are extra cues that let your rottie know whether he's supposed to move with you or stay in his place.

Positive Method

Heeling on leash starts with learning the heel position. Use a treat to lure your rottie into heel position at your left side. When he stands or sits at your left side, give him a treat. Use a one-word command, such as "Heel" or "Place."

Once your rottie has learned the heel position, clip the leash on his training collar. You should hold the leash loosely in your left hand and put the excess leash in your right hand.

Hold a treat in your left hand. Say, "Fido, heel," and start walking, left foot forward. If your rottie forges ahead, lags behind, or moves out of heel position, use the treat to lure him back to heel position. When you stop, put your rottie in a sit and give him a treat.

Clicker Method

Clip a leash on your rottie's collar. Wait for him to stand or sit at your left side, then click and treat. He may wander around again, but once he is on your left side, click and treat. It may take a few times for him to remain standing at your left side, but once he does, you're ready to teach him to heel. Use a one-word command, such as "Heel" or "Place." Start walking, left foot forward, and when he goes to the heel position, use the word "Heel" and click and treat. You'll follow the same procedure used for the positive method, but you'll click and treat your dog once he responds properly to your commands to heel and sit.

Stay

Many dogs find "Stay" more difficult to learn than other commands. Your rottweiler must know how to sit and down very well before you move on and teach him how to stay.

Positive Method

Put your rottie in a sit or down. Now, with a sweeping gesture of your open palm, bring your hand in front of your rottie's face and say, "Fido, stay!" Take a step with your right foot first.

 **Alert!**

Don't show any anger if your rottweiler breaks his stay. Simply put him back in it. You don't want him to break his stay because he is apprehensive or fearful.

If your rottweiler follows you, tell him, "No, Fido, stay!" Put him back in his original stay position. When you get him to stay for a few seconds, release him with an "Okay," and then praise him and give him a treat.

Increase the duration of the stay behavior by giving your rottie a treat while he is still in the stay. Wait a few seconds, then go back and give your rottweiler the treat. Quietly praise him. "Good stay!" If he stands up, gently put him back in stay position. You can gradually increase your rottweiler's time in stay.

You can increase time or distance, but not both at the same time. If your rottweiler breaks his stay, start with short intervals and short distances away from him and work your way up. Don't increase the time or distance until your rottie is reliable staying at the current time and distance.

Clicker Method

Put your rottie in sit or down. Do not click and treat. Now, with a sweeping gesture of your open palm, bring your hand in front of your rottie's face and say, "Fido, stay!" Take a step away with your right foot first.

 **Essential**

Always end your training sessions on a positive note. If your rottie is having trouble learning something, have him perform a command he does know, and then play with him a while before ending the session. Keep training upbeat and positive.

If he follows you, tell him "No, Fido, stay!" Put him back in his original stay position. When you get him to stay for a few seconds, release him with an "Okay," and then click and treat. Don't show any anger if he breaks his stay. Simply put him back in position. You don't want him to break his stay because he is apprehensive or fearful.

Increase the time by waiting a little longer and then click and treat. While he is waiting for the click and treat, quietly praise him with "Good stay!" If he stands up, gently put him back in stay position. You can gradually increase your rottweiler's time in stay.

You can increase time or distance, but not both at one time. If your rottweiler breaks his stay, start with short intervals and short distances away from him and work your way up. Don't increase the time or distance until he is reliable staying at the current time and distance.

Teaching Tricks

Now that you know a little about how to use the clicker, you might want to teach your rottie a few fun tricks. You'll need a clicker and a target stick for teaching tricks. Just about any trick can be taught with the clicker. Your rottweiler is willing to learn what you want—all you have to do is break the trick down and teach it in its fundamental components, and then put them back together. For example, if you want to teach your rottweiler to get his leash from the cupboard, you'll have to teach him to open the cupboard, pick up the leash, nose the cupboard closed, walk over to you while carrying the leash, and then hand you the leash. You must train each of these actions first and then put them together into one fluid behavior.

 **Essential**

Here are some words of advice on tricks. As fun as these tricks are, you can teach the wrong things to your rottweiler. Never teach him how to open doors unless he's an assistance dog. The refrigerator door should be forbidden. "Speak" is fun, but you can end up with a noisy rottweiler. And the bell ringing can cause you to go batty!

It is easy to get carried away while working the clicker, but dogs get tired of learning, too. Give your rottie a break, and let him rest if he's getting particularly frustrated with trying to learn. Put the clicker up and try something fun, like a walk or a game of fetch.

Shake Paw

Shaking hands, or "Paw," is often an easy trick to teach, especially with a clicker. If your rottie already knows the target stick, you can hold it in your hand and tell him to "Paw it," then click and treat.

If he doesn't quite get what you want, you can pick up his foot, then click and treat. Do this a few times until he starts giving you his foot. When he does, click and treat. Now, add the command, "Fido, paw," at the same time he offers you his paw, click and treat. After a few practice sessions, he'll have that trick down.

Bark on Command

This is a noisy command and not something you necessarily want your rottie to do all the time. But it makes for a fun trick. The trick to teaching your dog to bark on command is to wait until rottie barks, then click and treat. He may be so surprised that he barks again, or he may not. Wait for the next time he barks, and click and treat. Your rottie may suddenly catch on and bark. With each bark, click and treat. Now, add a cue word. "Speak!" is a good one.

Ring the Bell

Actually, this isn't a trick, but a useful housetraining aid. Whenever you let your rottweiler out, point to the bell with your target stick, and when he touches it, click and treat. Or you can gently cause him to nudge the bell each time you let him out. Soon, he'll be ringing the bell each time he needs to go out.

Go Get "Something"

This trick is actually quite useful. Start with the item of interest. (Choose your item carefully—it will be slobbered on and may have teeth marks on it. Sometimes to get your dog to hold the thing, you must smear it with peanut butter.) Show your rottie the item and get him interested in it. Click and treat when he mouths it. Do this several times. Give your dog a cue for the item: "Keys," "Leash," or "Bowl."

When he holds the item for a few seconds, give him the cue word and click and treat. Do this several times. Now, drop the item on the floor. Say the name of the item. If he mouths it or picks it up, click and treat.

Once you've gotten him to pick up the item, see if he'll continue to hold it as he follows you. Click and treat him if he follows you a few feet. Practice this a few times. Now, place the item in a visible place near your dog. Say its name and watch. Your rottie should pick it up. If he needs encouragement, try putting some peanut butter on the item. Click and treat when he picks it up. Do this several times. Stand close by and call your rottweiler to you. If he drops the item, give him the cue name again. Click and treat when he carries it to you. Gradually increase your distance from him.

Wave Goodbye

This is a simple trick that cues off the target stick, but it is still impressive. Start by putting your rottweiler in a sit. Hold the target stick high and say, "Paw." If you've taught this command, he'll reach up to touch the target stick. Keep doing this. Once he has made the connection between cue and behavior, substitute the cue word "Wave." Click and treat every time he paws the target stick. Then, slowly fade out or remove the target stick.

 **Essential**

Fading out a lure is sometimes tough and can take a long time. Switch between using a lure and using just your hands. As your rottie becomes used to simply performing the motions of a behavior, you can start fading those cues out, too.

Give Me a Kiss

When your rottie licks you, click and treat. (Watch out, you may have your face scoured by the end of this training session!)

Each time your rottie kisses you, click and treat. Now, add the cue word "Kiss" or "Kiss me" before you click and treat.

Close the Door

This can be a dangerous one, if your doors automatically lock behind you, but it can also be helpful. Use the target stick on a partially opened door. Tell your rottie to "Touch." When he touches the door and the stick, click and treat. Continue this for a little bit and then switch to the cue, "Door." Continue to click and treat every time he touches the door.

Now, you must teach him to push the door shut. Give him the command "Door" and wait. If he touches the door enough to move it a bit, click and treat. If not, wait until he does. For each movement, from the barest movement until he pushes the door and makes it close, click and treat.

 Fact

"Beg" is a cute trick. Have your rottie sit. Now, use either a treat or a target stick above his nose to lure him to a beg position. Click and treat. Do this a few times and add the cue word, "Beg." As he gets the hang of begging, start phasing out the visual cue.

Dead Bug

You can do this one of two ways. The first way is to wait until your rottweiler is lying on his back. Click and treat the behavior. If you can't wait, put him in a down. Lure him to roll over onto his side, and click and treat. Do this several times. Next, lure him to roll over onto his back. Click and treat. Practice this several times. Now, add the cue "Dead bug" so that your rottie can connect the behavior with a command. Click and treat. Fade out the lures, and click and treat each dead bug performance.

CHAPTER 15

Teaching Manners

YOUR ROTTWEILER WILL BE A JOY to own if he understands the rules of the house. The problem that most dog owners have is that they haven't sufficiently taught their dogs what they expect from them. The people expect one set of behaviors, but the dog does what comes naturally. This causes a great deal of conflict between dogs and people. In this chapter, you will learn the simple commands that can help establish good manners in your rottie. Like the previous chapter, it provides both positive reinforcement techniques and clicker training methods, where appropriate.

Setting Rules

The groundwork for good behavior in your rottweiler comes from communication between you and your dog. Unfortunately, most owners speak bad "dog," and as a consequence, most dogs don't have a clue what their owners actually want. It is tempting as a dog owner to think that your dog is doing a certain behavior just to spite you. However, this kind of thinking is often mistaken, as what you are doing is anthropomorphizing the dog's behavior. The owner thinks up punishments intended to fit the crime, but the dog just doesn't seem to "get it." So, the owner thinks the dog is doing this to spite him.

Dogs don't feel guilty the way people do when they're caught. When you catch a dog doing something bad, he's likely to act submissive because your body language and tone of voice suggests that you're displeased. Dogs don't think in terms of "right" or "wrong." Instead, they think in terms of what causes good things or bad things to happen. Even so, they may not associate a punishment with a behavior. For example, your rottie will not understand that you withheld his food as punishment for chewing your shoes.

Bad Dog or Bad Owner?

Dogs don't set out to be bad. Most dogs behave inappropriately because the owners never communicated properly with them and then punished them for things they didn't know they had done wrong. This causes the dog to misbehave out of frustration. He may try several different behaviors in an attempt to figure out what you want, or he might repeat the same behavior because he doesn't understand the punishment.

 **Essential**

Once you set the ground rules for your rottweiler, don't let him get away with something "just this once." Dogs have an extraordinary memory when it comes to breaking rules. If you let him up on the bed once, he'll come to expect it. What's worse, once he knows that he can break rules and get away with it, he'll try again.

"I know he knows he's done something wrong!" the owner shouts. "Look at him! He *looks* guilty!" The problem with statements such as this is that dogs don't *feel* guilt. Guilt is a human emotion. The dog, anticipating a punishment from an angry owner (he can read body language very well) or expecting a punishment whenever the owner comes home (no, he doesn't associate your chewed-up shoes with the punishment), acts *submissive,* which is a dog behavior.

Setting the Ground Rules

So if punishment doesn't work, what does? Being consistent in your training and setting rules—that is, setting rules that your rottweiler can understand and learn. For example, if you don't want your rottweiler to chew your $200 pair of shoes, you must not allow him to chew your son's old sneakers. Your rottie cannot differentiate between the two. Before you allow your rottie to do something, think of the ramifications. Chewing an old sock may lead to chewing laundry. Chewing a piece of firewood may lead to chewing furniture. Mouthing your hands may lead to biting later on. Sitting on a chair may lead to raiding the table or counter. Opening the refrigerator to get a bottle of water can lead to raiding the refrigerator. Setting rules and enforcing them consistently are the keys to training a well-behaved dog.

 **Fact**

Some owners think that their dogs should come with some sort of preprogrammed knowledge of what is expected of them. Without training, your rottie is in essence an immature wolf, with most of the behaviors associated with a wolf. If you invited a wolf to your house, how would you expect it to behave? Don't expect your rottie to come hardwired with house-manner expertise.

Think about what you're willing to allow versus what isn't appropriate. If you allow your rottie to jump up on you when you're wearing your old sweatshirt and blue jeans, you're also allowing him to jump up when you're in your business suit. You're also allowing him to jump up when your friends come by. Think your actions through. If you allow your rottie to sleep on the old sofa, what happens when you get a new sofa?

Before you get angry at your rottie, look at what you've done to cause the behavior. Have you given him full control of the house without properly training him? Is he bored? Does he really understand the rules?

▲ **Don't let this soft demeanor fool you. Rottweilers are known for their great strength, athleticism, and loyalty.**

Teaching Good Habits

It is easier to teach good habits than train out bad ones. If your dog doesn't have the chance to be bad, chances are that he'll still be good even if a golden opportunity to misbehave comes his way. Dogs are creatures of habit. They love routine, and they look forward to having everything orderly in their lives. If you've kept your rottie confined at home, the time that the gate is accidentally left open, he may decide that staying around home is a better idea than running loose.

Watch Me

Okay, so now you understand that you must be consistent in your training, and you must teach good habits first. What sort of training do you do? The first useful command is the "Watch me!" command. This command is excellent in training but also in situations where you must get your rottie's attention quickly, such as in competition or perhaps in a crowded area. "Watch me!" strengthens the bond between your rottie and you.

Dogs generally won't make eye contact with another dog. Making eye contact is often considered challenging or aggressive. When you initiate eye contact with your rottweiler, you're teaching him that you're in command of the situation. Once your rottie accepts this, it is comforting to him and gives him the assurance that you're the one who will lead.

 Essential

Pick one word for a command and stick with it. Don't confuse your rottie by changing commands. This will only serve to frustrate both you (as you aren't getting the behavior you want) and your dog (as he is unsure of what you want him to do).

"Watch me!" is great for keeping your rottweiler's attention focused even in the most confusing circumstances. Practice "Watch me!" everywhere you can with your rottie so that you can use it when there are a lot of distractions.

Positive Method

To teach "Watch me," start with a treat, such as a bit of cheese or luncheon meat. Hold the treat up between your eyes and say, "Watch me!" Holding the treat in such a way will help keep your rottie focused on you and not on distractions. When your rottweiler makes eye contact, even for a second, toss him the treat and praise him. Work on this a few times and again as you teach him other commands.

Clicker Training

Hold your clicker and wait for your rottie to accidentally make eye contact, then click and treat. Again, wait for him to make eye contact and click and treat. As he figures out that he's being clicked and treated for making eye contact, the behavior will continue. Add the keyword, "Watch me!" with the eye contact, and click and treat.

Go to Your Bed

Your rottweiler's bed may be his bed or his crate, depending on how you wish to train for this. This is a great command when you need to put your rottie in his crate or if you want him to stay on his bed while you vacuum, bring groceries in from the car, or greet houseguests.

Positive Method

Show your rottweiler the treat and lead him toward his crate or bed. Toss the treat into the crate or onto the bed with the command "Bed!" Praise him as he goes to his bed to get the treat. You can either work on this a few times or do this whenever you have him go to his bed for the normal routine.

 Essential

You may notice that some commands are actually two or more commands combined. This is the basis for teaching dogs. You break the command up into elementary parts, and once your dog has mastered each part, you put them together.

Once your rottie has mastered going to his bed, the next step is to teach him to stay if he isn't in a crate. If your rottie is to remain on his bed (and his bed isn't a crate), put him in a down position and tell him to stay. Have him stay for a few seconds, give him a treat, and then wait for a few seconds more before releasing him with the "Okay" command. Slowly work up to longer periods of time, as you would when teaching "Stay."

Clicker Method

Whenever your rottie goes to his crate or his bed, click and treat. Use the command "Bed" in association with his going to his bed. You may first have to lure him into the crate or onto the bed with a treat. Toss the treat into the crate or onto the bed with the command "Bed!" Click as he goes to his bed to get the treat. You can either work on this a few times or do this whenever you have him go to his bed for the normal routine.

Once your rottie has mastered going to his bed, the next step is to teach him to stay if he isn't in a crate. If he is to remain on his bed (and his bed isn't a crate), put him in a down position, click and treat, and tell him to stay. Have him stay for a few seconds, click and treat, and then wait for a few seconds more before releasing him with the "Okay" command. Slowly work up to longer periods of time, as you would when teaching "Stay."

Stay Off the Furniture

Most people abhor dog fur and muddy paw prints on their sofas and chairs. Even if you don't, you should probably not allow your rottie to lie on the furniture because it increases his status in his mind. You should never allow a dog to sleep on the bed with you. It raises him to your equal.

Conventional Method with Positive Training

When you see your rottie beginning to jump up on the furniture, tell him, "No! Off!" Don't yell, just tell him. You may have to move him to the floor or, if he is too big, use a treat to lure him off the furniture. "Off" means four paws on the floor. When he obeys, have him sit, and give him the treat. It is much harder to keep a dog off the furniture when you're gone, so it is advisable to put your rottweiler in his crate.

 **Fact**

You can also use the clicker to train this behavior. When you see your rottie beginning to jump up on the furniture, tell him, "No! Off!" Move him to the floor using the target stick, and click and treat. "Off" means four paws on the floor. When he obeys, have him sit, and click and treat.

Leave It

Sometimes your rottie will be interested in something that you don't want him to be interested in. It could be a piece of trash on the ground, another dog, a cat, or a person. "Leave it" is an excellent command to keep your rottie from getting into something he's not supposed to.

Conventional Method with Positive Training and Clicker Method

When your rottweiler shows interest in something that he shouldn't, you should try to redirect his attention. Try "Leave it," followed by the command, "Watch me!" If you've been successful with your "Watch me!" training, your rottie should turn his attention to you from the item of interest. Give him a treat (or click and treat, if using the clicker).

But sometimes the item is too interesting. At that point, you will have to get your rottie's attention. If he's on leash, tell him, "No, leave it!" Don't yell or shout; he can hear you just fine. Pull him away from whatever it is that interested him. Show him a treat and give it to him once you have his attention (or click and treat if you are using the clicker). If your rottie is off leash, you may have to show him something more enticing and clip a leash on his collar to lead him away.

Teaching "Leave It" with Positive Methods

You can teach "Leave it" at home with certain items. Plant a "Leave it" item—something that would be interesting but not harmful if your rottie got hold of it. (Don't use his toys or food you would normally give him.) Put some Tabasco sauce or Bitter Apple solution on the item in question. Have your treats ready for "Watch me." When your rottie expresses interest in the item, tell him, "No, leave it." Then follow it up with, "Watch me!"

If he ignores your command and picks up the item, he'll have a nasty surprise. If it is coated with something he dislikes, he'll drop it. Show him a treat and have him perform "Watch me!" Give him the treat and praise him.

 Fact

Most behavioral problems stem from a lack of communication or miscommunication between the owner and dog. Once you're able to show your rottie what is the correct behavior, he's more apt to do the correct behavior than to do the negative behavior.

Try again with other items that are tempting but not dangerous if he mouths or eats them. Again, coat them with a bitter solution or Tabasco to be sure to make them unappetizing when he touches them. He'll associate the words "Leave it" with leaving things alone that look appealing but really aren't.

Clicker Method

You can teach "Leave it" at home with certain items. Plant a "Leave it" item—something that would be interesting but not harmful if your rottie got hold of it. Of course, don't use his toys or food you would normally give him. Again, put some Tabasco sauce or Bitter Apple solution on the item in question. Have your treats ready for "Watch me." When your rottie expresses interest in the item, tell him, "No, leave it." Then follow it up with, "Watch me!" Click and treat when he makes eye contact.

If he ignores your command and picks up the item, he'll have a nasty surprise. If it is coated with something he dislikes, he'll drop it. Click and treat when he drops it. Then have him do a "Watch me!" after which you click and treat.

Try again with other items that are tempting but not dangerous if he mouths or eats them. Again, coat them with a bitter solution or Tabasco to be sure to make them unappetizing when he touches them. He'll associate the words "Leave it" with the need to leave things alone that look appealing but really aren't.

Trade

If your rottie has something in his mouth that you don't want him to have, you must take it from him. But grabbing something out of a big dog's mouth can be a risk, especially if you didn't raise him from puppyhood. A less threatening approach is to use the command "Trade." "Trade" tells the dog that you will give him something very yummy if he lets go of whatever he has.

The only way to teach "Trade" is to prepare for it. You first must find out what is absolutely irresistible to your rottie and be very stingy with it. Liver, fish, cat treats, bits of hardboiled egg, peanut butter, and certain types of sandwich meats, like liverwurst, may be good choices.

When you see your rottie chewing a toy, go up to him and hold out the delectable treat and say "Trade!" If he catches a whiff of his favorite food, he may drop the toy (click and treat, if you're using the clicker). At the same time you reach for the toy, give him the treat, so he is occupied. Hold the toy for a few seconds and then give it back. Praise him!

This does two things. First, it teaches your rottie that you'll give him something tasty if he lets you take it. Second, if the item is acceptable, you'll give it back to him.

 **Question?**

What if your rottweiler won't leave it or trade?
In rare circumstances, you may have to insist that you take the item away or keep your rottie away from it. Try anything you can to break his attention away from the interesting thing (with food, commands, or even correction, if necessary). Clip a leash on his collar and lead him away.

No Chew

Part of the challenge of owning a dog is teaching him what is appropriate to chew and what isn't. All dogs, including rotties, chew. You can't stop that behavior, but you can redirect it to appropriate items. This requires that you have plenty of dog chews and toys available for your rottie to chew.

The "No chew" command works a lot like "Trade." When you catch him chewing on something inappropriate, you must tell him, "No chew!" and then offer to "Trade." This time, however, the trade item is a toy or chew that is acceptable. Praise him or click and treat when he takes the item and allows you to remove the offending item.

If he refuses to take the toy or chew in exchange, you may have to do a trade with an irresistible treat and then rub the toy or chew with some of the treat so that he gets some pleasure out of that. Otherwise, you may have to search for some toys or chews that are irresistible.

No Dig

Some dogs are naturally inclined to dig. Some dig out of boredom or because they want to cool off, but many just enjoy digging. If your rottie is an excavator, you may have trouble trying to break him of this habit.

 **Alert!**

> Never leave your rottie outside all day by himself. There's too much trouble he can get into, such as digging, barking, and terrorizing the meter reader. Boredom is a bad thing, too. He can become a Houdini dog without too much effort.

Look at his holes. Is one in a place where you can sacrifice a bit of lawn or garden so he can have a place to dig? If so, fill all the other holes with his feces and put dirt on top of them. Then wait until he starts digging in the appropriate hole. When you see your rottie digging where he's supposed to be, praise and treat him (or click and treat). Give him the command "Dig" to associate his digging behavior with that one spot. Continue to fill up the other holes with his feces and dirt. Dogs hate digging through their own feces so this will be a discouragement. See Chapter 17 for further information on stopping digging. Ⓔ

CHAPTER 16

Socialization

SOCIALIZATION IS VERY IMPORTANT for your rottie. If he isn't socialized, he can become fearful or aggressive in new situations and when meeting new people. It is important to have a well-socialized dog because he'll react appropriately in everyday situations.

Why Socializing Is Important

Socializing your rottweiler is very important nowadays. With breed bans and people becoming more litigious, an aggressive dog has no place in society. If your rottweiler becomes fearful or aggressive in what most would consider normal situations, he is a liability. An untrained and unsocialized rottweiler can be a hazard.

 **Alert!**

Be very careful socializing your rottweiler around children. Be sure that he is only exposed to good kids who understand that rottweilers can feel pain. Keep him away from kids who torment or tease dogs.

The good news is that you can socialize your rottie. Socialization requires that you spend time with your rottweiler, exposing him to as many situations as you possibly can. The more encounters he has with people, places, and things, the more pleasant he will be to be around.

▲ Introducing your rottweiler to other dogs is an important part of socialization.

Places to Socialize Your Rottweiler

You can socialize your rottweiler in the following places:

- Dog-training classes
- Trips to the pet-supply store
- Trips to the vet and the groomer
- Trips to friends' houses
- On walks around the neighborhood
- In dog parks
- At fun matches (practice for dog shows)
- Outside the grocery store or shopping center
- At outdoor cafés
- In car trips to the drive-through windows at banks and fast-food restaurants

These are a few of the many places you can take your rottweiler. Be creative! While there are many places that don't allow dogs, many others don't mind a pooch or two showing up. As a rule, anyplace that has food or serves food won't allow you to bring your rottweiler inside because of health department regulations, but that doesn't mean that you can't opt for outdoor seating at the local coffeehouse.

Puppy Classes

The first place your rottweiler should be socialized at is puppy kindergarten, or KPT. This class allows puppies younger than six months to meet with other puppies and their owners in a positive environment. KPT allows the puppy time to interact with the other puppies and people and learn that what might appear to be a scary situation is actually harmless. Puppies also learn some rudimentary commands. A KPT class is normally six to eight weeks long. All puppies should go through KPT after they receive their vaccinations.

Socializing with People

When you go to visit friends and relatives, don't forget to take your rottie! If your friends and relatives like dogs, there isn't any reason you shouldn't take your rottweiler along. It is a great way for him to meet people and perhaps other animals.

Preparing to Visit Friends

Before you do take your rottie, make sure that your friends can accommodate him. Your rottie should know rudimentary commands (see Chapter 14), and he should be comfortable with meeting people if this is a long visit. Before you go, exercise him so that he'll be a little tired when he meets your friends. A rottweiler with a lot of rambunctious energy won't make for a fun visit. If you can, arrange to go see your friend for a short time. Your friend should not be afraid of rottweilers and perhaps be a dog owner herself. When you're first visiting, just do so to meet and perhaps have a snack.

 **Essential**

If your friend owns a dog, don't arrange for the dogs to meet the first time. This is already quite a bit of excitement for your rottie, and you want the encounter to go well. Don't expect a long stay at this point. Use plenty of praise and treats (or click and treat appropriate behaviors).

If Your Rottie Is Nervous

If your rottie acts a little shy, put him in a sit and have a cup of coffee or tea with your friend and just talk. Let your rottie get used to her presence without pushing him to interact. If he's still nervous at the end of your meeting, just play with him a bit and then take him home. You may have to have several visits before he decides it is okay to be friends. After your visit, take your rottie for a long walk or play with him for being such a good dog.

▲ In addition to being calm and confident, rottweilers are also known for being somewhat aloof or reserved in character at first, especially with strangers.

More Socialization

The more places you take your rottie, the more people he will meet. Instead of walking him in areas where he won't see too many people, try walking him near shops or parks where he can see people interact. If at any time he becomes nervous or upset, try "Watch me!" or other commands so that he focuses on you and not on being nervous or upset.

 **Alert!**

Be very careful to watch your rottweiler in any new encounter. Don't force the encounter if he is shy or agitated—he may bite out of fear. If anything becomes too difficult for him to handle, remove him from the situation and give him some time to recover and relax.

Whenever someone approaches him, don't tighten your leash. Tightening is often a signal for your rottie to become nervous or aggressive. If he doesn't do well with people petting him yet, inform the would-be petter that he's a little anxious around other people and that it's not a good idea to pet him right now.

In almost all cases of socialization, if your rottie isn't used to a particular situation or is acting fearful, it is best for you to expose him to it a little at a time. For example, if he thinks that children are scary, walk him on the other side of the street of a school when school is at recess so he can watch the children play without having to interact with them. Use "Watch me!" and other commands to focus his attention on you and not on the children. If you're using a clicker, click and treat for desirable behavior.

Socializing with Kids

Children seem to cause the most concern for dogs. Their erratic movements and loud noises tend to make a dog nervous if the dog isn't used to children. Introduce teenagers first when introducing your rottie to children. Once he is okay with them, slowly move to younger ages. Be sure to find well-behaved children who understand that they shouldn't yell and scream or make sudden movements around him so he won't be scared.

If at any time your rottie growls, correct him. A quick "No!" is usually all that you need to stop the growl and to stop whatever you or the other person is doing to cause the growl. If your rottweiler continues to show aggression, you should take him to a professional animal behaviorist or trainer who specializes in aggression.

◀ Rottweilers make loyal companions to their owners and enjoy contact with other dogs, too.

Socializing with Other Pets

Some rotties don't tolerate other dogs well, but others will. When you introduce your rottie to other pets, do so on neutral ground— at a dog park, on a walk, in a regular park, or someplace where neither dog will feel like defending his turf.

It is best to introduce dogs on leashes so if there's any aggression, you and the other owner can quickly pull the two apart. Watch the dogs as they interact. If the dogs hold their tails straight up and move them slowly, walk stiffly and tiptoe, raise their hackles, or begin to snarl, separate them immediately! These are the first signs of aggression. However, play bows, wagging tails side to side, a submissive posture, and sniffing are all forms of greeting and, in some cases, play behavior.

 **Alert!**

Don't allow your rottweiler to associate with aggressive dogs. Aggression can be a learned behavior, and all it takes is a fight or two to convince your rottie that other dogs are mean.

When introducing your rottie to cats or pets other than dogs, consider putting your rottweiler in a sit/stay and using the "Watch me!" command. If you use a clicker, click and treat whenever your rottie focuses on you instead of the cat or other pet.

Becoming Accustomed to New Situations

New situations can be scary to your rottweiler if you haven't exposed him to them. For example, if your rottweiler is a country dog, he's likely to be overwhelmed by a walk in New York City. Likewise, a dog from Manhattan might be shocked to see a herd of cattle. While you can't prepare for every possibility, you can expose your rottie to as many new experiences as possible. With each new experience, he becomes used to seeing more new and unusual things. When he finally does see that herd of cattle crossing in front of your car on a road trip to Texas, he may be a little surprised and even excited, but he's not frightened, intimidated, or aggressive.

 **fact**

Fourth of July, New Year's Eve, and Halloween can be very stressful for your rottweiler. The loud noises and people dressed in costumes can be frightening if he isn't ready for it. Before Halloween, you might want to buy a mask and show it to your rottie before putting it on so he can see it is you and not some weird person.

So what sort of experiences should you expose your rottie to? Certainly, you should start with those situations he's likely to experience in his life: trips to the groomer and veterinarian; riding in a car; meeting strangers and children; meeting other pets; seeing people in various types of clothing, such as winter or summer clothing and raingear like umbrellas; seeing squirrels, deer, or other wildlife; holidays like Halloween and Christmas where there is a lot of noise and people; fireworks; and visiting other people's homes. You may also want to expose your rottie to experiences he may not have often—visits to the ocean, forests, or mountains; visits to the city, where he may not be allowed everywhere but is allowed outside; trips to the boarding kennel; and other places.

Visits to the Veterinarian and Groomer

Visiting the vet and groomer can be stressful for your rottie. Your can make them less stressful by getting him used to the things that will happen to him at either of those places.

If your rottweiler is used to being examined and groomed, he's less likely to become agitated when the vet examines him or the groomer brushes him. The better behaved your rottweiler is, the more likely he's going to be treated better. Keep him on a leash at all times and don't let him socialize with any of the other dogs. Some are sick, and many don't feel well enough to be friendly.

You can also make this an enjoyable trip. First go to the vet, and then take him to the park or the pet-supply store for a treat. This way, your rottie will naturally expect that there will be something good to look forward to after the vet or the groomer. You can also go to the vet's office just to pick up medications or visit the groomer to say hi and take along your rottie. He will learn that trips to the vet or the groomer aren't bad all the time and therefore shouldn't be looked at with anxiety.

◀ Every dog needs a break for some fun.

Riding in the Car

Lots of dogs despise riding in the car. Part of the reason for this is the motion. The other reason is that most dogs only get in the car to go to the groomer, the boarding kennel, or the vet. If you had that option, you too wouldn't enjoy riding in the car.

You can, however, make riding in the car an enjoyable experience. First, be certain that your rottweiler is secure, either in a crate or in a car harness before you start the car. A loose dog is not only a danger to himself if you get in an accident, he can also cause an accident if he gets nervous or underfoot.

 **Essential**

Like people, some dogs ride in vehicles better than others. If your rottie gets motion sickness, your vet can recommend the appropriate dosage of over-the-counter medication to combat the ailment.

Start by taking your rottie to fun places in the car. Hiking, matches, training, and the dog park are all fun places to go. Stop by the local fast-food drive-through and order a burger plain without anything on it for your rottie. He will soon tolerate, if not love, the car.

If you're planning a long trip in the car, be sure to take water and snacks and plan on rest stops. Your rottie will appreciate your thoughtfulness.

Baby in the House

Having a baby in the house does not mean relegating your rottie outside or to the basement. However, it does mean that it's time to take certain precautions. Never leave your rottie alone with the baby at any time. He may be curious and knock over the crib or, if the baby is a toddler, knock over the toddler.

Your rottie will naturally be curious about the new addition to the household. Don't hold the baby where your rottweiler can sniff or lick at him, but rather, work with him on his commands such as "Watch me!" and on his sit/stay and down/stay. Have someone in the household spend extra time with your rottie if you are busy with the baby. If no one is available, consider hiring a dog walker to come by and play with him so that he isn't feeling neglected.

Your baby will not know whether he's hurting your rottie, so it is best to keep his little fingers away. Your dog will no doubt love the baby once he throws strained beef on the floor!

Dog Park Etiquette

Dog parks are a great place for dogs to run free and socialize, but your rottweiler should be friendly with other dogs before you take him to a dog park. The dog park may be large or small, or it may be a fenced-in part of a larger park. Regardless, be sure to bring enough bags to pick up your rottie's poop so that you can help keep the dog park clean.

Dogs generally don't exercise themselves in a dog park—they need human interaction. When you go into a dog park, see who's there before unclipping your rottie's leash. Some dogs are friendly, but some are not. If your rottie hasn't met a particular dog at the park, you might want to talk to the owner and introduce the two. If, at any time, your rottie or the other dog shows aggression, clip your leash on and move to another area of the park. If the park is small, you may want to look for another park or simply walk your rottie on leash instead.

 Fact

Some dogs do very well at dog parks, while others don't. If your rottie is happy just to play with you or if he is friendly with other dogs, then you can enjoy the park. But if your rottie is aggressive toward other dogs, forgo the dog park or go at times when there aren't any other dogs.

Never turn your rottie off-leash in a regular park, and always clean up after your dog defecates. Be a responsible dog owner, and you'll help open up more parks to dogs; being irresponsible will contribute to getting dogs banned from more areas.

Moving to a New Home

Regardless of whether you're moving across the street or across the country, you should take your pets with you. Years ago, people didn't move with their animals, especially those who were in the military and who couldn't always bring pets to their new homes. In these times, there's no good reason for leaving your pet behind. Moving does not mean finding a home for your rottweiler. After all, do you find homes for your children when you move?

Moving can, however, be a stressful time. Your rottie will no doubt notice the packing and preparation. He'll feel your stress as you try to prepare for your move. It is important to take time to exercise him and make sure you don't neglect him.

Moving day is hectic and you can't always keep a close eye on your dog. As the big moving day arrives, you might want to consider boarding your rottweiler or having him stay at a friend's house while the movers do their work. This will reduce the stress plus prevent a possible escape due to an accidentally open door or gate.

Traveling

If you're moving across the country and are driving, look for pet-friendly hotels. Although there are many motels and hotels that allow pets, some have size restrictions, so be sure to contact the motel or hotel you'll be staying at. Hotels and motels do change management and policies frequently, so be sure to ask. Motel 6 and KOA Campgrounds usually allow dogs when no other place will.

 **Alert!**

Don't try to "sneak in" your rottie. Most hotel owners are savvy at spotting pets, and you may be charged extra or may lose your room or the room rate for trying to sneak in.

If you're traveling by air, be sure to contact the airline and tell them you'll be traveling with a dog. Airline regulations change frequently, so be sure to get the more up-to-date information from the airline.

Arriving at Your New Home

Once you arrive at your new place, your rottweiler will be excited. Let him explore the new place, but watch him carefully. Some dogs like to mark their new place, and your rottie may forget his house manners. Be very careful for the next few weeks until he learns that this is your new home. If he gets out, he will be lost and confused.

Spend extra time with your rottie after you move. Place his bed and toys in a special place and show him where they are. After a little while, your new home will feel like home to both of you.

▲ Rottweiler puppies should be eager to explore their environment.

Behavioral Problems

AS WONDERFUL AS THE ROTTWEILER IS, there are rotties with behavioral problems. Behavioral problems fall into two categories: those that are biological, and those that are a reaction to something within the environment. It is up to you to determine which category your rottie's bad behavior falls into.

Identifying the Root of the Problem

This chapter deals with problems that are caused primarily by lack of training or by allowing a small problem to get out of hand. Many owners fail to see the slippery slope of a single action. They let the problem escalate to intolerable limits before they actually do something. Remember, it is easier to teach good habits than correct bad ones, so if you're looking at this chapter in the hopes of a quick fix, you won't find it here. Your rottie has taken time to learn this annoying behavior, whatever it is, and you're not going to fix it overnight.

Biological or Behavioral?

Before looking within these pages for a correction, look at the behavior itself. Could there be a possible underlying biological cause for this? For example, if your rottie is whining and crying when he's in his crate, could he be uncomfortable due to a joint problem? Or if he growls and snaps at you when you approach his food bowl, does he have a condition that makes him ravenous? You can't really know unless you have your vet look at him and see if there is a biological cause for the behavior.

 **Fact**

There are no quick fixes once a bad behavior starts. It can take weeks or even months before you correct a problem behavior once it has been ingrained. It is always better to prevent bad behavior than it is to try to correct it.

When you take your rottie to the vet, talk to your vet about the behavior. Ask your vet if there could be any underlying biological cause. Make suggestions. Vets aren't infallible, and they may not have thought the entire problem through. For example, if your rottie is suddenly urinating everywhere, don't accept that he just might not be housebroken—ask the vet if he might have a condition such as Cushing's disease, diabetes, or a kidney disease. Has your rottie been drinking frequently? (All that urine has to come from somewhere!)

Behavioral Causes of Bad Behavior

If your vet has determined that there is no apparent biological cause to your rottie's bad behavior, the next step is to determine the behavioral cause. Bad behavior usually has a root cause in the owner's behavior. Often, the owner doesn't see that allowing a certain behavior will eventually lead to the one they find obnoxious. For example, it is cute when a puppy mouths your hands. But as the puppy mouths, he learns that it is acceptable to chew on people, and as his bites become harder, it becomes a real problem. If you teach him right away that he should never have his teeth on flesh, this natural tendency of his won't develop into a biting problem.

Look at the current behavior and ask yourself if there is something you're doing that might be contributing to your rottie's delinquency. Often it's the little, apparently harmless transgressions that escalate into others.

 **Essential**

If you're having a behavioral problem and your rottie is intact, spay or neuter him. While it won't solve all the problems, it will help if you aren't fighting against hormones too!

Some bad behavior stems from excess energy and boredom. How would you feel if you were cooped up in the house all day and all night with nothing to do? That excess energy gets released one way or another, and it's up to you to channel it where it's least harmful. Many pet owners find their dogs' behavior problems magically disappear when they become involved in dog sports or give their rottweilers a job to do. A tired dog is a happy dog and one less likely to get into mischief. Exercising your rottie or giving him a job to do will help curb his excessive energy and make him a better pet.

Are You Causing the Behavior?

When you see a problem start, look at what you're doing as an owner. Are you treating your rottie like a dog or treating him as if he's in charge? You can do things to establish your role as owner.

Free feeding is not allowed. Have scheduled mealtimes. Don't just dump food in a bowl and let your rottie eat whenever he feels like it. He must know that the food comes from you. You do this by establishing feeding times. Make him earn his treats. Treats and snacks are okay, but don't give them to your rottie just because he exists. Make him sit, lie down, or perform a trick.

Your job as owner is to establish dominance over your dog, so make sure you do not act as one of his littermates. If your rottie is sleeping in your bed, put him in a crate in your bedroom. Sleeping with you makes him think he is your equal. Never play tug-of-war or roughhouse games. It puts you on his level. When the two of you leave the house or pass from room to room, you are the first one through each door. Never allow your rottie to "mount" you or loom over you. It makes you look like a subordinate. If you eat dinner the same time as your rottie, eat first and then feed him.

 **Alert!**

Never tolerate aggression in your rottie toward people and other dogs. An aggressive dog is a liability. Contact an animal behaviorist who specializes in aggression so that you can correct this serious problem.

Exercise your rottweiler vigorously. As stated before, a tired dog is a happy dog and one less prone to mischief. Practice sit/stays and down/stays. Spend five minutes a day practicing commands. This isn't much time out of your busy schedule, and both you and your rottie will benefit from it. You could also take up a dog sport such as flyball, agility, or herding.

Barking and Whining

Dogs bark at everything—and nothing. Some dogs are so prone to barking that they bark to hear themselves bark. (Kind of like some people who can yak for hours.) But excessive barking is more than a mere nuisance. In many municipalities, you can be hauled into court for having a dog that barks excessively. If your rottweiler is barking and keeping the neighbors up at night, or if he's barking outside during the day, why are you leaving him outside? He's better off indoors in his own crate than out disturbing the neighbors.

If your rottie is inside and is still barking and whining, you can use a squirt bottle filled with water or pennies in a pop can to discourage him from whining while you're home. When your rottie carries on in his crate, toss a pop can with some pennies in it at the top of the crate so that it makes a loud noise but doesn't hurt him. (Make sure the pop can has been crinkled so the coins don't fall out of the can into your dog's crate.) You can also use a squirt bottle filled with water and give him a quick spray when he whines. Don't yell or even tell him no. If you can give the correction without letting him see you, so much the better.

 **Essential**

If you choose to shake the pennies-in-a-pop-can as a method of correction, make up several and keep them nearby in places where you may need them. Remember, you need to correct your dog immediately following the bad behavior or he won't understand.

But what about when you're away? In these cases, a citronella bark collar might work. This bark collar uses a fragrant citronella spray that activates when the dog barks. Dogs dislike the spray and will avoid barking so that they don't get sprayed.

Chewing

Is your rottweiler chewing on inappropriate items or being destructive? Does it happen when you're not home or when you are home but can't watch him? Is there a particular item your rottie is interested in, or does he choose random things? Is he a puppy and teething?

Chewing Basics

Chewing is normal for dogs, especially puppies. If your rottie is teething, then chewing is normal behavior. You'll have to provide acceptable chew items and crate him when you cannot watch him.

If he is an adult, have your vet look into possible tooth problems, such as puppy teeth that haven't come out or adult teeth that haven't grown properly.

If the problem isn't biological, you need to put your rottweiler in a crate when you leave or when you can't watch him. The crate will keep your rottie from destroying your house. Give him an appropriate chew item for those times when you're home but are unable to watch him every second.

Curbing Destructiveness

You may want to consider tying, tethering, or umbilical cording—these are all different terms for the same type of training. Get a long line or rope (about ten feet) and fasten one end to your rottie's collar. Tie the other end to your belt loop. Now your rottweiler has no choice but to go where you go and follow your lead. This is a wonderful tool, and it works well in most problems involving house soiling and destructive chewing. Your rottie will be unable to run off and chew something up without your seeing it. This accomplishes two things. First, it helps prevent destructive behavior. Second, it helps bond your rottie to you. It makes him focus on what you're doing instead of what he wants to do.

 **Fact**

Most people encourage begging behavior by giving their dogs treats while they're eating. The first thing you must do is stop giving your rottweiler table scraps while you're eating. The second is to enforce a down/stay during dinner. Use clicker training or positive reinforcement to keep your dog in a down/stay while you eat.

Don't leave your rottie loose alone in the house all day. You're saying to him, "Here are your toys!" Naturally, your rottie is going to take advantage of that. When you do catch your rottie chewing something inappropriate, offer an appropriate item as a trade, such as a chew item or rawhide. This will help break the cycle in chewing, but it takes a while.

Digging

Dogs dig for various reasons. Some do so out of boredom, while others dig to escape. Still others just enjoy digging. Digging is a tough habit to break. It is natural for a dog to enjoy digging. If there's a place in your backyard where you don't mind a hole or two, leave those alone. Fill the other holes with your rottie's feces, and cover them with dirt. Allow your rottie to dig in the places you haven't filled in.

▲ **It's hard to imagine this rottweiler puppy growing into an adult!**

You can further discourage digging when you're home by using the pennies-in-a-pop-can method. This requires you to watch your rottie while he's outside. When he starts digging, hurl a shaker can in his direction (but don't hit him!). If you can do this without his seeing you, he will be impressed. After a few times, he'll associate unpleasantly loud rattle things with his digging. Obviously, this method only works if you're home. If your rottie is outside while you are gone, you will have to bring him inside and crate him or have a special kennel run where he can dig.

Fear of Loud Noises

Some dogs suffer from fear of thunder or other loud noises. This fear seems to get worse with age, and the dog doesn't get over it. Lightning storms are not the only time for loud noises, though. Loud celebrations like those for the Fourth of July, New Year's Eve, and even Halloween can be frightening to your rottie.

 Alert!

Don't keep your rottie chained outside. Most dogs become frantic during thunderstorms and may try to escape. Dogs have choked to death by catching their chains on fences.

If your rottie is terrified of loud noises, keep him inside in a crate during thunderstorms and during celebrations such as the Fourth of July. Dogs that are afraid of loud noises are likely to try to escape and may try to hurt themselves. Dogs have been known to jump out of closed second-story windows in sheer panic. If your rottweiler continues to become panicked or fearful even when crated, talk to your vet. Your vet may be able to prescribe medication that will help calm him.

Jumping Up

Rottweilers that jump up on their owners or others are usually excited or happy to see the person. Put your rottie in a sit when you come in the door, and crouch down to pet him. Don't pet him unless he is in a sit position. He'll soon learn that the only way to get your attention is to sit nicely.

An alternative method to keeping a dog from jumping up is to bring your knee up and letting him bounce off it with a "No, off!" correction. The problem here is that most dogs find that fun to bounce off and back on again. You can try this method, but teaching him to sit to be petted is often more effective.

Mouthing and Nipping

Some rotties are just naturally mouthy dogs. They can't help it—they want to mouth your hands or arms or whatever they can reach. But those big jaws can bruise or cut into you.

If you haven't taught your rottweiler that teeth on flesh is a no-no, start teaching him now. A quick flick of the forefinger on the nose, or holding your rottie's lower jaw for a few seconds when he tries to nip usually sends the message. Use the words "No bite!" Your corrections must be timed right for it to work.

 **Esseñtial**

Those rotties that come from Schutzhund lines can be especially mouthy. (Protection work requires biting.) If you've gotten with a dog out of Schutzhund lines, it may take a while to train out the mouthing.

If you're unable to make the necessary corrections, find a stuffed toy or a ball that is special to your rottie. Make it his toy to carry around when he's in the house, on walks, and everywhere when he's with you. If his mouth is filled, he can't nip. Eventually, that nipping will stop because he's learned a new behavior.

Separation Anxiety

Some rottweilers become anxious and destructive when left alone. If your rottie destroys or chew things or whines and cries when he's left alone, he may be suffering from separation anxiety.

Sometimes, but not always, separation anxiety has behavioral causes. You may unknowingly be causing separation anxiety in your rottweiler. Do you make a big production out of leaving and arriving? Do you act as though you are going and never coming back? Keep your exits and arrivals as low key as possible. You may have to spend a few days desensitizing your rottweiler to your comings and goings by taking short trips out of the house and then returning.

Crating your rottweiler will stop the destruction, but it won't stop the whining and crying. Some dog owners like to leave the radio or television on for background noise. If you do decide to try this, choose music stations with soothing music (light jazz, classical) or stations with calm voices (the Weather Channel is excellent). Talk radio often features argumentative chatter, which will only heighten your rottweiler's anxiety. If he continues to display separation anxiety, talk to your vet. There are medications that will help separation anxiety.

Scavenging

If your rottie constantly steals food and other items off the counter, you're going to have a tough time breaking him of this habit. Every time he steals, he gets a reward (food or the item he stole), so his action reinforces itself.

 **Fact**

Occasionally a trick backfires. Be careful what you teach your rottweiler. Some dogs can open cabinets and refrigerator doors because their owners thought it'd be a neat trick. The problem is, dogs are quite clever and recognize a good thing. Keep your refrigerator and cabinets off limits to your rottie.

Once the stealing starts, it is very hard to stop it for good. After all, your rottweiler has received a great reward for stealing something. It may take months or even years to break the cycle. If you slip up, and your rottweiler steals food (or trash) again, you're back to where you started.

To correct this problem, you must remove the temptation first. Keep all food out of your rottweiler's reach. This may require that you install child latches on your cabinets and hide your dinner in the oven or microwave when you leave it unattended.

Most owners of garbage raiders learn to hide their trash under the kitchen sink or behind closed doors. If your rottweiler is particularly adept at trying to get at items on the stove, either crate him or use static mats. These are low shock mats that give a jolt similar to walking across a carpeted area and touching a doorknob. (They're unpleasant, but harmless.) Most dogs avoid these mats after one or two encounters. After that, you can leave the mat turned off or use a "dummy" mat. You should only use static mats as teaching tools in situations where your rottie could be seriously injured. Taking items off the stove could burn your rottie, and therefore, the static mats are justifiable.

The worst thieves actually figure out how to open the refrigerator and help themselves to what's in there. Again, childproof straps or latches may be in order to keep your rottweiler out of your refrigerator. ⓔ

CHAPTER 18

Competitive Obedience

I F BASIC OBEDIENCE IS A BREEZE for you and your rottie, maybe you should consider competitive obedience. In competitive obedience, you're judged on how well your rottweiler performs in the ring. The good news is that competitive obedience is run in a set program. The bad news is that it is not as easy as it looks. Dogs frequently make mistakes, and one little mistake in the obedience ring may prove costly enough for a non-qualifying score. In this chapter, you'll learn the basic routine of novice competitive obedience. You'll also learn the titles your rottweiler can earn if you choose to go beyond the novice ring.

Novice Competition

So, you think your rottweiler is good in obedience? If so, you can take your rottie's training to the next level by working toward competing in obedience. At AKC obedience trials, you and your rottweiler can compete against other purebred dogs for placement and even the "High in Trial" award—the equivalent to "Best in Show" in the obedience world.

Purebred Competitions

Any purebred dog registered with the AKC can compete in AKC trials. If your rottweiler isn't registered with AKC or he is a rescued dog, don't despair! He can obtain an indefinite listing privilege

(ILP) number from the AKC. AKC allows ILP registered dogs to compete in obedience and other competitive sports. Both AKC and UKC have their own versions of obedience. Both intact and neutered/spayed dogs can participate in competition obedience.

 **fact**

Novice, open, or utility? A or B? The jargon can get a little abstract when you talk obedience. If this is your first time entering an obedience trial, or if you've never put an obedience title on a dog, you should enter at the Novice A level. Novice B is for those trainers who have already put a title on one of their dogs.

The purpose behind the obedience competition is to earn a qualifying score at a trial. A qualifying score is 170 or above. Any dog can qualify. In fact, all dogs at the trial could theoretically earn qualifying scores. However, the pressures of competition put an extra burden on the dog and handler when they compete.

How Obedience Trials Are Run

There is a set routine for all obedience trials. At the novice level, the dog is required to heel on leash in a pattern, heel on leash in a figure eight, perform a stand for examination, come on recall, heel off-leash, perform a long sit, and perform a long down.

The obedience judge awards points for each exercise in novice obedience. The following is the maximum amount of points a judge can give for each exercise in the obedience trial:

- Heel on leash and figure eight: 40 points
- Stand for examination: 30 points
- Heel free: 40 points
- Recall: 30 points
- Long sit: 30 points
- Long down: 30 points

Earning Legs

Once your rottie qualifies in one competition or trial, your dog is said to have "earned a leg." Your rottweiler earns an obedience title by obtaining three qualifying legs under at least two different judges in obedience competition. For instance, your dog could achieve his CD, CDX, and UD titles.

 **Question?**

What do the letters stand for in titles?
Those titles you will likely come across include CD (Companion Dog), CDX (Companion Dog Excellent), UD (Utility Dog), OTCH (Obedience Trial Champion), and UDX (Utility Dog Excellent).

Training for Novice Competition

Before you decide to enter your first novice competition, you should enter a training class specifically developed to train your dog for the novice ring. In this class, you'll learn proper obedience handling. You'll be able to train with other dogs and have your rottie become accustomed to strange surroundings and dogs. Classes frequently set up mock trials that help you train for the real thing.

Even though you should train with a class, you still need to work with your rottweiler at home on the various novice exercises. Practice makes perfect, and if you're planning to compete for advanced titles such as UD, OTCH, and UDX, your rottweiler is going to have to be nearly perfect.

The good news is that most obedience and breed clubs offer fun matches for obedience and conformation practice. At these fun matches, your rottweiler can experience the flavor of the obedience trial without having it count. At many fun matches, the "judges" allow you to train your dog, make corrections, and use the experience to discover how well your training is going.

Heeling on Leash

Your rottweiler should already know the heel position (see Chapter 14). In heeling on leash, you demonstrate control over your rottweiler while walking. Your rottweiler must walk in heel position at your side and adjust to your pace, whether it is fast, slow, or normal. He must also watch you closely so he turns left or right, or about-faces with you. When you stop, your rottweiler must sit straight in heel position.

To train for this, move your rottweiler into the heel position on your left side. Use a clicker or a treat to get him to be precise in his position. Then hold a treat in your left hand. Tell your rottie "Heel," and start walking, left foot forward.

 **Essential**

Always start heeling by starting out with your left foot forward. Dogs see the left leg movement before the right leg moves. This becomes another signal to your dog that he is to move with you.

Don't allow your rottweiler to forge ahead or lag behind you. Instead, use the clicker or show him the treat to lure him into the correct position. When he is in the correct position, praise him, and give him a treat or click and treat.

Turning

You'll need to work on turns. When you do, you may have to exaggerate your leg movement at first so your rottie will see that you're turning and will turn with you. When you stop, you may need to give a "Sit" command so that he will sit each time you stop. When you stop, have your dog sit in the heel position, and give him a treat or click and treat.

In the Ring

When in the ring, the judge will give you commands that will tell you which way you must go and how fast you must walk. These commands include the following:

- **About turn:** The handler and dog must turn around and continue in the opposite direction.
- **Fast:** The handler must run and the dog must accelerate appreciably to maintain the heeling.
- **Forward:** The handler must go forward in a straight line.
- **Halt:** The handler must stop and the dog must sit straight in heel position.
- **Left turn:** The handler and dog must turn left.
- **Normal:** The handler and dog must resume their normal pace.
- **Right turn:** The handler and dog must turn right.
- **Slow:** The handler and dog must slow their pace to less than normal.

Figure Eight

Figure eight is a lot like heeling on leash, except your rottweiler must heel on leash around two obstacles. The obstacles are actually ring stewards, who are there to assist the judge. Unlike heeling on leash, there are only two commands: forward and halt. Your rottweiler must sit when the judge calls out "Halt!" and you stop.

 **Fact**

The trick to success in obedience is not just training—socialization is important, too. Your rottweiler will be much more at ease if he's comfortable in strange environments. Dog shows and obedience competitions are about as strange as environments come!

You and your rottweiler must walk in a figure-eight pattern without the dog lagging or sniffing. Figure eights are tricky because you cannot adapt your pace to your rottie's pace or you will receive a nonqualifying score. Likewise, you can't jerk your dog forward. When training for figure eights, you need to encourage your rottweiler around the obstacles and slow down for the straight sections. In this way, your rottie learns to maintain one speed at all times.

Stand for Exam

After performing figure eights, the next exercise is stand for exam. This is a version of stand/stay, where you stand your rottweiler in heel position, remove his leash, and give him a stay command. You then walk six feet in front of your dog and turn around. The judge walks over and allows your dog to sniff her hand and then touches your rottweiler on the top of the head, on the back, and on the hindquarters. Your rottie must not break his stay or move even a paw while in stay. The judge instructs you to return to your dog, and then the exercise is complete.

 **Essential**

When you put your rottie in stay and then walk away, always step with the right foot forward. Dogs see the left leg movement before the right leg moves, so if the right leg moves first, you've already taken a step before the dog sees it. Also, it becomes another signal to your dog that he is to stay where he is.

Training Stand/Stay

Training for stand/stay is a little more difficult. Your rottweiler should have learned sit/stay and down/stay through normal obedience training before tackling this command. Stand your rottie at heel position with a leash on, and give the "Stand" command. Then give him the "Stay" command. Now, walk forward (right foot first!) and turn around directly in front of him. If he breaks his stay to follow you, tell him, "No! Stand. Stay," and put him back in his stand. Stretch out your hand with a long sweeping motion and put your hand in front of his nose as though you are telling him to stop.

This may take several times to get the stand/stay right. Once your rottie stands, return to heel position, release him with "Okay" and praise him. Practice this several times until he is comfortable holding a stand/stay at a close distance.

Training for the Examination

Next, teach your rottie to accept touching from strangers. If you haven't already socialized your rottie, do so now. Have a few friends approach your rottweiler slowly and allow him to sniff their hands. Then have them lightly touch your rottweiler on the head, back, and hindquarters. You may need to distract your rottweiler by giving him a treat as they touch him. Your dog will be so occupied with eating the treat that he won't be nervous that someone is touching him. Eventually, he'll associate the exercise with a good thing—getting a treat—and will not be nervous when a stranger touches him.

 Fact

A complex command is taught by breaking it into a series of simple commands. For example, a dog that hasn't learned stay won't usually stay at a distance because he isn't comfortable with the stay command close up. Once you teach him stay, you add complexity by either increasing the time he must hold his stay or the distance.

Lengthen the Distance

Next, you'll need to increase your distance between yourself and your rottweiler. Continue to perform the same exercise, only one or two feet away. As your rottweiler becomes more reliable, you may practice without a leash. Again, build up the distance slowly. If, at any time, your rottie becomes nervous or starts breaking his stays, drop back to a previous distance where he didn't break his stay and practice with that for a while before increasing the distance again.

The Recall

The recall or come command is the next exercise. You must put your rottweiler in a sit/stay off-leash, turn around, and walk to the opposite side of the ring. Then, on the judge's order, you must call your rottie. He must come straight to you and sit straight in front. The judge will then give the command "Finish." Your rottie must perform a finish—that is, he must either go around you or turn around in place so that he will be in the heel position.

 Alert!

The obedience ring has a very strict protocol. You can't use food in the obedience ring, nor can you give a command twice. You can't use training tools, such as the clicker. You can't scold your rottweiler there, either. Likewise, you can't use hand signals and voice commands together, except when putting the dog in a stay.

Your rottweiler will need to know how to come. If he doesn't come reliably, teach him now. When you begin teaching the recall, hold a treat in your mouth to bring your dog up to a perfect sit in front of you. Some people use raw liver, but if you can't bear the thought of having raw liver in your mouth, cheese and cold cuts work just as well. If the notion truly disgusts you, just hold a small piece between your teeth. You don't have to look like a chipmunk squirreling away nuts in your cheek pockets!

When your rottie comes straight up to you and sits (be careful not to drop the treat if you have to give the sit command!), drop the cheese as a treat when he sits perfectly.

Finishing your rottweiler is more difficult. Start by using a treat to lure him into the correct position while using the command "Place," "Heel," or "Finish." When he follows the treat correctly, give him the treat and praise him.

Off-Leash Heeling

Off-leash heeling is the same as heeling on leash, except that now your rottweiler is not under your direct, physical control. The judge's orders are the same as those he gives for heeling on leash. Don't work your rottie off leash until his on-leash heeling is perfect.

Train in an enclosed area for off-leash work, especially at the beginning. Otherwise, if your rottweiler decides to bolt, you may have trouble getting him back, and then he will have learned a new trick—one you don't want!

You may want to attach a very light line made of parachute cord or fishing line when you start off-leash heeling. Take off your rottie's regular leash and keep the light line loose. Now, practice heeling without the leash as you would if the leash were still attached. Use treats as you normally would to keep your rottie focused on heeling, rather than the freedom of being off the leash. Do not use the light line unless your rottie tries to bolt. In that case, you can use the line to stop him from running away.

The Long Sit

The long sit is performed as a group exercise. This means that at the judge's discretion, all competitors perform the exercise together. After the long sit comes the long down. Your rottweiler must sit quietly next to other dogs that are also performing the long sit. You must sit your rottie while in heel position and give him a stay command. Then you turn and walk to the opposite end of the ring, where you stand while the judge times the long sit. The dogs must sit for one minute.

 Essential

While this may be a competition, it can still be a lot of fun! Don't become so competitive that the experience isn't fun for you or your rottie. Keep in mind that your rottie can pick up on your emotions. If you are tense, chances are he will be too. If you are having fun, then so is he.

Dogs that break the long sit receive no points for that exercise. As the time approaches one minute, the judge will tell the handlers to return to their dogs. At this time, you must return to your rottie, walk around him, and stand next to him so that he is in proper heel position. The judge will then tell you when the exercise is complete.

Teaching the long sit requires that your rottweiler know sit and stay. Build up to longer stays, but stay close to your rottweiler. As he becomes comfortable with the longer stays, gradually lengthen the distance between you and your rottie.

If, at any time, your rottie becomes nervous or starts breaking his stays, drop back to a previous distance where he didn't break his stay. Practice at that level of difficulty for a while before you increase the distance again.

The Long Down

Like the long sit, the long down is performed as a group exercise, meaning that at the judge's discretion, you and all other handlers must wait for the dogs to perform the long down. This exercise occurs immediately after the long sit. Your rottweiler must lie quietly next to other dogs that are also performing the long down. You must put your rottweiler into a down while he is in heel position and give him a stay command. Then you turn and walk to the opposite end of the ring, where you stand while the judge times the long down. The dogs must lie quietly for three minutes.

Dogs that break the long down receive no points for that exercise. As the time nears three minutes, the judge will tell the handlers to return to their dogs. At this time, you must return to your rottweiler, walk around him, and stand next to him so that he is in proper heel position. The judge will tell you when the exercise is complete.

 **Fact**

Once you start stacking up the titles, you'll need to learn how to write your dog's name. Obedience titles—CD, CDX, UD, and UDX—appear after the dog's registered name. OTCH appears before the dog's registered name.

Teaching the long down requires that your rottie know down and stay. Build up to longer stays, but do it while staying close to your rottie. As he becomes comfortable with the longer stays, gradually lengthen the distance between you and your rottie.

If, at any time, he becomes nervous or starts breaking his stays, drop back to a previous distance where he didn't break his stay and practice with that for a while before increasing the distance again.

The Canine Good Citizen Test

Dog bites and dog attacks have been in the forefront of the news lately. You've probably heard about how a child has gotten mauled by a dog or someone has been seriously bitten or even killed. These attacks seem to be growing in number.

Municipalities have stepped in to try to prevent such tragedies, but ironically, this blanket punishment tends to affect those with well-behaved dogs. Breed bans are meant to curb dog aggression. However, these breed bans don't address the real problem, which is irresponsible ownership. Sadly, rottweilers are one of those breeds the government tries to ban.

If you've been training your rottie, you and your friends know that your rottie is a good citizen—but how does anyone else? There is a way, and that's through the Canine Good Citizen test (CGC). Training facilities and fun matches often offer CGC testing for a nominal fee. Some trainers have whole courses devoted toward obtaining your dog's CGC.

What Is the Canine Good Citizen Test?

In 1989, the AKC decided to proactively promote responsible dog ownership with its Canine Good Citizen test. Those who train and show dogs understand that it is not the breed that's the problem, but the individual dogs. By creating the Canine Good Citizen test, the AKC created a test that would showcase particular dogs as model citizens. This is a series of temperament and obedience tests designed to show that the dog that receives his CGC title is an outstanding member of the canine community.

Any dog, purebred or mixed breed, may test for his CGC. The test is pass or fail. Dogs may take the CGC test until they pass. Your rottie must pass a series of ten tests in order for him to receive the CGC title. These tests include the following:

- **Accepting a friendly stranger:** The dog must show no fear when someone strange approaches his owner and talks to him or her.
- **Sitting politely for petting:** The dog must accept petting by a stranger when the dog is with his owner.
- **Appearance and grooming:** The dog must accept being brushed gently by the evaluator and allow the evaluator to pick up each foot and examine his ears. The dog is also judged on whether the dog is clean and groomed.
- **Walking on a loose lead:** The dog must walk on a loose lead and walk with the handler including turns and stops.
- **Walking through a crowd:** The dog must walk through a crowd of people without pulling, jumping on people, or acting fearful.

- **Sit and down on command and staying in place:** The dog must sit and lie down on command. The dog must then stay in place while the owner walks twenty feet away and returns to the dog. The dog may change position, but he must stay in the same place.
- **Coming when called:** The dog must wait while the owner walks ten feet and then calls him. The dog must come to the owner.
- **Reaction to another dog:** The dog must show no more than a casual interest in another dog as that dog and his handler approach the first dog and his owner.
- **Reaction to distraction:** The dog must show no fear when faced with two everyday distractions. The dog may show curiosity, but not aggression or shyness.
- **Supervised separation:** The dog must accept being left with the evaluator for three minutes while the owner is out of sight.

Chapter 19

Advanced Training

I N THE PREVIOUS CHAPTERS, we focused primarily on obedience training. But not all competition is obedience. For instance, you can show your rottweiler in the conformation ring. You can teach him to herd. You can teach him to track or have fun in agility. All these fun sports are open to your rottie. Rottweilers also have a serious side. They can work as therapy, assistance, and search and rescue dogs, too. Let's take a look at the versatile rottie and what he can do.

Conformation

When people talk about dog shows, they're often talking about conformation dog shows. Think of the Westminster Dog Show, and you're looking at the top AKC conformation dog show. Or, if you'd like, think of the funny movie *Best in Show*.

Once a dog that wins points goes to the best-of-breed ring, he goes up against the winner of points of the opposite sex and against dogs that are champions. In this competition, there are a number of awards he can potentially win: "Best of Breed" (best dog there, male or female), "Best of Opposite Sex" (the opposite sex of the winner of the Best of Breed), or "Best of Winners" (the best of the two dogs that took points).

Judging

In any case, conformation is a judging of how well the dog conforms to standard (remember the rottweiler standard in Chapter 1?). Dogs are judged according to how closely they conform to their standard. What makes conformation so interesting is that it comes down to the judge's interpretation of the standard.

Most rottweilers don't fit the standard and have one or more faults or flaws that prevent them from ever winning in the show ring. This doesn't make these dogs substandard as pets. In fact, many rottweilers that don't fit the standard make excellent pets and/or obedience, agility, and tracking dogs.

Some of the standard is quantitative, such as height or number of teeth. But much of it is qualitative—what is medium length when one looks at the head? The forehead line should be moderately arched—what is a moderately arched forehead? A serious fault is a male dog that looks feminine (bitchy dog) or a female dog that looks masculine (doggy bitch)—who decides that a female dog looks masculine instead of feminine? See the problem?

 **Fact**

Dog shows aren't a casual affair. Those in the audience dress up to go to dog shows. While in the ring, handlers wear nice outfits to look good to the judge and to complement their spiffy dogs.

In the ring, the judge has the handlers gait their dogs once around the ring. Then, the judge examines each dog, looking at his bite, head, and topline and feeling his legs. On the males, the judge will examine the dog's testicles to make certain that both are fully descended. Then, the judge will ask the handler to gait the dog in a pattern: up and back, L-shaped, or a triangle. The judge will then ask the handler to gait the dog to the end of the line.

A dog that might be chosen as a winner by one judge may be panned by another. Handling is as much an art as a science because a good handler can emphasize the dog's outstanding qualities while de-emphasizing flaws. Much of dog shows has to do with handling and not necessarily the dog himself.

Show Classes

In conformation shows, the showing classes are divided into the following categories:

- Age group: puppy 6 to 9 months; puppy 9 to 12 months; 12 to 18 months (young dog)
- American Bred
- Bred By (for the breeder/owner)
- Open

In these classes, males compete against males and females compete against females. The winners of each of those classes compete to be "Winners Dog" or "Winners Bitch," in which the dogs compete for points. The winner in each class goes into the best-of-breed ring.

The best-in-breed winner may earn anywhere from one to five points toward the championship. The amount of points awarded depends on the number of dogs the winner had to beat. A win is called a "major" when it earns three points or more. When the dog has earned fifteen points, including two major wins, the dog becomes a champion and may put the initials "Ch." in front of his name.

You might wonder how a dog becomes the "Best in Show." Once the dog wins best of breed, he continues to compete in the group class. In the rottweiler's case, the best of breed must compete against all the other best-of-breed dogs in the Working Group. If the rottweiler wins this class, he is awarded "Best in Group," and he goes on to compete for best in show against all the winners of the various groups.

Grooming for Conformation

Part of the trick of conformation showing is grooming your dog. The good news is that unlike those fluffy or time-intensive breeds that require scissoring and special grooming, the rottie is a wash-and-wear kind of dog. His coat should be coarse, so a little top coat dressing that emphasizes its coarseness can be used. Some handlers trim the rottie's whiskers for a more refined look, but you don't have to do that.

Training for Conformation

Training for conformation isn't as easy as grooming. There are entire books devoted to conformation handling. Your best bet is to find a professional training center that teaches conformation classes and handling. Finding a mentor is also an option.

In these classes, you'll learn how to stack your rottweiler. Stacking is sort of like posing your dog so that he stands in a position that is most flattering to him. When a handler stacks his dog, he emphasizes his best qualities and hopefully hides the negatives. Stacking requires that the dog accepts your moving his feet until he's in the position you want. Some dogs free-stack, meaning they've been trained to come into that position automatically.

 Essential

Unlike obedience and agility, in conformation competition you get to use food treats in the ring as much as you want. In fact, the judges and other handlers expect you to.

You can train your rottweiler to stack by putting him into a stand/stay and baiting him (that is, holding a piece of liver or cheese in front of his nose). Very carefully, move your rottie's feet so he is standing squarely. When he stays there, give him the treat. If he stays in the correct position, you have a stacked dog.

Professional Handlers

It takes a while to learn to handle a dog correctly. In many circumstances, owners hire professional handlers to show their dogs in conformation shows. Hiring a handler is expensive work. Most charge $50 each time they step into the ring. So, if your rottie ends up competing for best in show, you're probably paying over $200 by the end of the first day.

This is why it is important to choose a good handler. Most people find their handlers through word of mouth. They know someone or have watched someone handle other people's dogs. If you're looking for a handler for your rottie, ask your breeder or a trainer. Sometimes trainers will handle dogs professionally.

If you do decide on the handler route, be aware that you may be sending your rottweiler away to compete in shows outside your area. Some people hand their dogs off for months at a time to obtain their championships.

Herding

Although most people don't think of the rottweiler as being a herding dog, the rottie can trace his roots back to the drover dogs in Germany. The rottie still has the instincts to herd animals, even though it might look a little odd seeing a big, powerful dog herding ducks, sheep, or cattle.

 **Fact**

Once you start looking, you'll probably find plenty of trainers who specialize in working with Border collies, but training rottweilers to herd is a vastly different job. Find a trainer who has trained rottweilers to herd to teach you.

Herding is quite popular, and there are four major sanctioning organizations for herding: the American Kennel Club (AKC);

Australian Shepherd Club of America (ASCA), which allows all herding dogs, not just Australian shepherds; International Stock Dog Society (ISDS); and the American Herding Breed Association (AHBA). We'll be focusing primarily on the AKC trials.

Training for Herding

Training for herding isn't easy if you live in a city or suburbs— it is tough to find a herd of cattle or sheep nearby, and your neighbors would probably complain about the noisy ducks! Still, there are places to train your rottie to herd. Most of these are out in the country, and the trainers keep sheep, ducks, or cattle so people can train their dogs on them.

▲ As part of advanced training, rottweilers can be used for herding animals.

Herding is partially instinct, but it is also training. Your rottie needs to know right and left and also how to go toward the herd and away from the herd. You also have to be able to call your rottweiler off the herd. These are the basic herding commands:

- Away to me: Run counterclockwise around the herd.
- Come (or go) to me: Run clockwise around the herd.
- Lie down: Stop or lie down.
- That will do: Stop herding.
- Walk up: Go behind the herd and drive them.

Contact one of the national organizations for information on clubs and trainers in your area. Once you find some prospective trainers, ask if the trainers have experience in training rottweilers. Not all breeds herd in the same way, and training techniques for one breed may not work with another.

Herding Titles

There are several different herding titles your dog may acquire. For the Instinct Tested certificate, the dog must show sustained interest in herding livestock. This means he either moves them ahead of the handler to drive them or goes around them, gathering them and moving them toward the handler—the dogs may also perform a combination of those methods. To obtain a Herding Tested (HT) title, the dog must pass the herding test under two different judges. This is not a prerequisite for participation in herding trials.

 **Alert!**

Warm up your rottweiler before any athletic endeavor. Start with a slow walk and progress to a trot for about ten minutes. Then help your rottie stretch by moving his legs in the entire range of his natural motion. Don't force or push on his joints, and don't have your rottie bend in any unnatural position.

To obtain a Pretrial Tested (PT) title, the dog must pass the pretrial test under two different judges. This is not a prerequisite for participation in herding trials. To obtain a Herding Started (HS) title, the dog must receive three qualifying scores under three different judges for the same course and livestock in started trials. The title will specify the course and livestock type after the HS designation.

To obtain a Herding Intermediate (HI) title, the dog must receive three qualifying scores under three different judges for the same course and livestock in intermediate trials. The title will specify the course and livestock type after the HI designation. The dog must have an HS before he can compete for an HI.

To obtain a Herding Excellent (HX) title, the dog must receive three qualifying scores under three different judges for the same course and livestock in advanced trials. The title will specify the course and livestock type after the HX designation. The dog must have an HI before he can compete for an HX. To obtain a Herding Trial Champion (HCh) title, the dog must have earned his Herding Excellent title and must have subsequently acquired fifteen championship points according to placement in the advanced class.

Tracking

Is your rottie a super sleuth? Can he follow a trail? Tracking is a complex sport in which dogs follow a scent and find items, called "articles," that the tracklayer leaves behind. AKC and UKC both offer tracking titles, and tracking is one of the three components of Schutzhund work and competition.

Training for Tracking

Any dog may learn to track, but the training is complex. It is important to find a trainer who understands how to train a tracking dog. Before you get started training your tracking dog, you must obtain certain items for tracking. You'll need a tracking harness, which is specially designed to allow your dog to move without restricting him; a tracking lead, a long line that you can use to control your rottie (the AKC requires twenty- to forty-foot tracking leads in competitions, but when you train, you may want a shorter one for more control); and tracking articles such as leather gloves or a leather wallet, though you'll also need items that are made of plastic, metal, and cloth later. Once you have these items, you're ready to begin training.

Follow these steps to train your dog to track:

1. Start by showing your rottie an article, such as the glove. Tease him with it and make it something fun to play with. Hide treats in it, and let him find the treats in it. The glove will be a fun thing, and your rottie will associate it with food. Use the word "Find!" whenever he touches the glove so he associates the word with the article.

2. Now, put your rottie in a sit/stay and fill the glove with treats. Take ten steps straight away from your rottweiler and drop the glove in sight. Turn around and walk back and tell him to "Find" the glove.

3. Your rottweiler should make a beeline for the glove. Praise him and give him treats. If he doesn't, lead him to the glove and praise him and give him treats.

4. Practice this until your rottweiler heads straight for the glove each time.

5. Now, vary the place you drop the glove. Keep dropping it in sight so that your rottie can see you leave the glove for him and get the treats. Some dogs will go to the first place you trained them to look for the glove but will then continue to the second place. Help your rottie find the glove if he's having difficulty.

6. Continue to "hide" the glove in many places until he understands that the glove can be in various locations.

7. Once your rottie is comfortable looking for the glove, put him in a place where he cannot see you hide it. Make a short track, drop the glove, and then walk back along that same track. Keep the distance under ten feet.

8. Take your rottie to the start of the track, and tell him "Find!" He may be confused. If so, lead him to the glove and the treats and praise him.

9. Continue to do this until your rottie understands that he is supposed to follow your track to find the glove and its rewards. You may have to leave a few treats along the track so he can figure it out.
10. Once he's comfortable with following the track, change the track so that you leave the glove in a different place.

This game of hide-and-seek provides the basis for tracking. Once your rottweiler becomes proficient in finding the glove, you have a second person, a tracklayer, move around a glove impregnated with her scent. After this, you can then begin lengthening the track. It all sounds very complex; but when broken into its simplest components, your rottweiler will learn the basics of tracking. Tracking tests take a very long time because the track must age. Still, if you enjoy it, waiting awhile won't deter you.

Tracking Titles

Now that you have a feel for tracking, you can get an idea how difficult it is to earn tracking titles. To obtain a Tracking Dog (TD) title, the dog must earn two TD legs. The articles used in this test must be a leather glove or wallet impregnated with the scent of the tracklayer. The TD tracking test also places many requirements on the laying of the tract itself. The track must be between 440 yards and 500 yards, with legs of at least 50 yards long, and it must be composed of three to five turns, of which two turns must be a ninety-degree angle. The track must be "aged" thirty minutes to two hours—that is, after the track is laid, you must wait thirty minutes to two hours before starting.

 **Fact**

If you want to advance your dog to be among the best of the best, you can work to acquire the Champion Tracker (CT) title. This title is awarded to dogs that have earned their TD, TDX, and VST titles.

To obtain a Tracking Dog Excellent (TDX) title, the dog must earn two TDX legs. Here, the articles used must be four dissimilar, small personal items of the tracklayer, with the exception of the last item, which may be a glove or wallet. In the TDX tracking test, the track must be between 800 yards and 1,000 yards long, with legs of at least 50 yards. It must have five to seven turns, of which a minimum of three turns must be at a ninety-degree angle, and the track must be "aged" three to five hours.

To obtain a Variable Surface Tracking (VST) title, the dog must earn a VST leg with two judges in agreement. In the VST tracking test, the articles used must be four dissimilar, small personal items of the tracklayer, which include a leather, plastic, metal, and fabric item. The track must be between 600 yards and 800 yards long and must consist of a minimum of three different surfaces, of which two must be devoid of vegetation (such as concrete or gravel). The track has legs at least 30 yards long, with five to seven turns, of which a minimum of three turns must be at a ninety-degree angle.

Agility

Agility is one of the most fun and fastest-growing dog sports. In agility, your rottie follows an obstacle course, running against the clock. He climbs over A-frames, wiggles through tunnels, and leaps over jumps. It is exciting to watch and even more exciting to participate in. Unlike obedience, agility is constantly changing and provides variety. Many dogs that hate the strictness of obedience love agility because while there are some obedience requirements, they aren't as strict. Any dog may participate in agility provided he is healthy and has no physical defects such as deafness or blindness.

Agility Organizations

Agility's popularity is evident by the number of sanctioning organizations. These include the AKC, UKC, ASCA, USDAA (United States Dog Agility Association), and NADAC (North American Dog Agility Council). Each has its own particular style when it comes to agility.

▲ Rottweilers can participate in a wide range of agility training exercises.

AKC offers a variety of titles in two categories: standard class, and jumpers with weaves. It allows only purebred dogs either with regular registration or ILP registration. NADAC offers a faster version of agility based on British rules. NADAC offers juniors' and veterans' classes as well as standard, jumpers, and gamblers courses. ASCA offers competition to all dogs under NADAC rules.

 **Fact**

Agility made its debut at the Crufts Dog Show in England in 1989. It was simply an entertainment demonstration, but it so wowed the crowd that it became a sport in no time.

UKC offers a version of agility based on control and preciseness. UKC offers Agility I, Agility II, and Agility III courses. UKC equipment varies considerably from AKC, NADAC, and USDAA in their Agility II division. USDAA offers a faster version of agility based on British rules. USDAA offers standard, jumpers, relay, and gamblers courses. USDAA offers a champion program and a slower performance program. It also offers a junior handler class.

Deciding on an Organization

With as many agility organizations as there are, you may wonder which one is right for you and your rottweiler. Your choice is mostly a personal decision as there are no "good" or "bad" organizations listed here. Each has its merits and shortfalls. USDAA and NADAC offer variety through their many classes. They are fast-paced and allow mixed breeds as well as purebreds. If you're interested in control rather than speed, UKC agility might interest you. If you want to earn AKC-recognized titles with your rottie, then the AKC format makes the most sense.

Your choice of organizations may depend on your locale. Some organizations may not be as prevalent as others. AKC and USDAA have larger numbers of trials throughout the United States, but they may or may not be prevalent in your area. Contact each national organization for agility clubs in your area.

 **Essential**

There are several "varieties" of agility, including jumpers or jumpers with weaves, gamblers, relay, and standard. You certainly won't get bored if you try all these fast-paced games.

Try out various organizations before deciding on just one. You may find that more than one style of agility fits both you and your rottweiler perfectly. In this case, you may have a multititled agility dog! Many agility handlers have put agility titles on their dogs from more than one organization.

Obstacles

Your rottweiler will need to learn how to negotiate the obstacles before you two can compete. Although some forms of obstacles vary, there are still obstacles that are common to agility. These include the following:

A-frame: The A-frame is made of two six- to nine-foot ramps that meet to form a structure with a peak at the center, three to four feet wide at its base. Your rottweiler must climb the A-frame to the peak and climb down it, touching the contact areas on the way down.

Closed tunnel: The closed tunnel has an opening at one end (usually a barrel) with an eight- to twelve-foot long chute made of silk or parachute cloth that lies flat at the other end. Your rottweiler will have to enter the open side of the closed tunnel and push his way through the chute to complete the obstacle.

Dog walk: The dog walk is a single plank that runs between two ramps. It is a tall obstacle, similar to a catwalk. Your rottie must climb up the dog walk, cross the plank, and descend the ramp, touching the contact points on both sides.

Hurdles: There are a variety of jumps, with or without side wings, that your rottie may have to jump.

Pipe tunnel or open tunnel: The pipe tunnel is a tunnel that can snake into various patterns. Most dogs love tunnels and your rottweiler will enjoy this fun obstacle.

Seesaw: The seesaw looks like a playground teeter-totter without the handlebars. Your rottie enters the seesaw on the downside, crosses the seesaw, and tips the plank. He must touch the contact zones on both sides.

Table: This is a square table that looks like a large end table that can be set to the various jump heights. Your rottie must hop on the table and sit or lie down on it, depending on the command.

Tire jump: This is a jump in the shape of a tire. Surprisingly, the tire is difficult for dogs because they must jump through instead of over it.

Weave poles: Weave poles are made of one-inch PVC. They are set up in groups of six to twelve poles placed anywhere from eighteen to twenty-five inches apart in a straight line. Your rottweiler must enter the weave poles and weave through them.

Finding an Agility Training Class or Club

Should you train with a professional agility trainer? Unless you wish to spend the money to purchase or build expensive agility equipment, the answer is probably yes. Professional agility trainers have spent the money to obtain agility equipment that you and your dog can use. You and your dog can learn agility correctly through a class and benefit from the trainer's experience.

Most agility training classes are offered through obedience trainers or training clubs. Ask your veterinarian, clubs that sponsor agility trials, or other agility handlers where there are good agility instructors. Once you obtain a list, visit those instructors while they are teaching a class. You should visit the training session without your dog to determine if you like and approve of the class and the trainer's style of teaching.

▲ Another example of agility exercises rottweilers can participate in.

There are two types of agility classes. Both types have their own sets of advantages. One is a regimented class, where everyone in the class works on a particular object or handling technique. The handlers learn a specific technique or obstacle from the trainer. This method is good for beginners and those who need to learn new handling techniques. The other is a drop-in-type class where the individual handlers work on whatever each person feels her dog needs practice with. This is good for those who need to practice certain techniques that they've already learned or work on an obstacle that the dog is having problems with. While beginners can learn new obstacles in this environment, it may be more difficult than learning in a regimented class setting.

 **Essential**

If you are just starting out, try an agility fun day to find out if agility is something you would like to do. Then look for a regimented class. You can always attend drop-in classes to work on practicing certain obstacles or new techniques you've learned.

As you and your dog become more proficient, look for a variety of classes in different facilities. You can learn different training techniques and gain different insights as to how to train your dog. Not only that, but your dog will become comfortable with different equipment and different settings—something he will need to do if he is at a trial.

Flyball

Flyball is a fast, competitive sport in which relay teams of four handlers and dogs compete against each other against the clock. Although not an AKC sport, it is sanctioned through the North American Flyball Association (NAFA), and your rottweiler may earn titles through competition. Flyball is almost as addictive as agility. Your rottweiler will have a lot of fun with flyball. It is fun to watch as well!

In this sport, each dog must jump over four hurdles to reach the flyball box. The dog triggers the box to eject the flyball, catches the ball, and then returns over the same hurdles to the finish line, where the next dog on the relay team waits to run the course. Dogs on the team earn one point for an aggregate time of less than thirty-two seconds. If the team's aggregate time is under twenty-eight seconds, each dog scores five points. If a team is under twenty-four seconds, each dog earns twenty-five points.

Any healthy dog can compete in flyball. The height of the flyball hurdles depends on the smallest team member. The hurdles are set four inches shorter than the smallest dog on the team, with a minimum height of eight inches and a maximum of sixteen inches. Your rottweiler will have to learn to jump sixteen inches, but if there is a small dog, he will only have to jump eight inches, which makes small dogs very popular team members indeed!

Flyball Titles

Dogs earn titles according to the amount of points accumulated. The following are NAFA titles:

- Flyball Dog (FD): 20 points
- Flyball Dog Excellent (FDX): 100 points
- Flyball Dog Champion (FDCh): 500 points
- Flyball Master (FM): 5,000 points
- Flyball Master Excellent (FMX): 10,000 points
- Flyball Master Champion (FMCh): 15,000 points
- ONYX Award (ONYX): 20,000 points
- Flyball Grand Champion (FGDCh): 30,000 points

Training to Catch the Flyball

Flyball requires a flyball box. Plans are available in flyball books and on the Internet, or you may purchase a flyball box from an obedience supplier. You will need four specially constructed flyball hurdles and tennis balls.

It helps if your rottie loves to chase tennis balls. Teach your rottie to catch the ball when you throw it and call him to you. Give him praise and treats when he catches it and brings it back. Use a command to catch the ball that you will use in flyball. Then start throwing the ball in the same manner as a ball would fly coming out of a flyball box.

Add the flyball box once your rottweiler is proficient at catching the ball. Step on the flyball box, and release a ball. Use the word associated with catching the ball in this new game. It may take a few times for your rottie to catch the ball, but if he knows the command to catch, he will get the idea.

 **Essentïal**

Anytime your rottie participates in an athletic activity, always take him for a walk to cool down and allow him to drink after the exercise. Also offer him water during any exercise. Dehydrated muscles can cause injuries.

To teach your rottweiler to trigger the flyball box, bring him to the flyball box. Take his foot and press it against the box to release the ball. Or you can use the clicker and a target stick and have him paw the box. Either way, give your rottweiler the command to catch before the ball releases. Your rottie may catch the ball as it shoots out if he's quick. Even if he does not catch the ball, give him a treat and praise him for stepping on the box. Keep repeating the action until your rottweiler gets the idea and starts catching the ball.

Teaching to Jump

When you start teaching jumps, start at the lowest you can possibly go, even though your rottie might be able to jump higher. Carefully lead him over. Use enthusiastic encouragement and the command "Over!" "Jump!" or "Hup!"

Once he is completely confident going over the jump, put a long line or tracking lead on your rottie's collar. Put him in a sit/stay and walk over to the opposite side of the jump while still holding the leash. Stand on the other side to the right or left of the jump and call him over. Gentle tugs and treats in your hand should easily guide him over the jump. Practice directing your rottie to the jump from a distance.

 **Alert!**

Be very careful what kind of surfaces your rottweiler jumps on. If it is hard or has uneven footing, it can cause injury. It is always better to try some shorter warm-up jumps first before having your rottie jump higher jumps.

Now, raise the bar. The bar should be the next level higher or a height at which your dog needs to jump a little to get over. Practice running him over the new height until he gets used to it. Then you can practice directing him to the jump. Once he is proficient at jumping at a lower height, you can raise the bar and practice at a new height until he is finally at the height he needs to be for competition.

Now, clip a long line to your rottweiler's collar and toss a tennis ball over the one jump. Have him retrieve it and call him back over the jump. Praise and give him treats for bringing the ball.

Putting Catching the Ball and Jumping Together

Start with one hurdle and add the flyball box. Give the "Over," command and then the flyball "Catch" command. Call your rottie back over the hurdle, and praise and reward him. It may take a little time at first to put all the commands together. If your rottweiler doesn't complete the command, break down each portion of the behavior into sections and slowly add each component.

Then, as he becomes proficient with one jump, add a second jump and send your rottie over the hurdles. Once he becomes proficient at that, add a third hurdle and train with that. You'll need to add one a hurdle at a time until your rottie is jumping all four hurdles, hitting the flyball box, and jumping all when returning the ball.

Therapy Dogs

Rottweilers may not always be thought of when one thinks of therapy dogs, but many rotties have made outstanding therapy dogs. You can find therapy dogs in hospitals, at nursing homes, and other care facilities, where they provide cheer and unconditional love to patients. The healing effects that pets have on patients amaze many volunteers who bring their dogs to these facilities. Dogs often have a way of helping withdrawn patients become less reclusive and more cooperative. Patients enjoy the dogs' nonjudgmental manner and often form special friendships with therapy dogs.

Any well-behaved dog may become a therapy dog. Your rottie should have obedience training and possibly pass a Canine Good Citizen or other temperament test. Many therapy dogs know a few tricks, such as shake paws or bark on command, to entertain the patients, but tricks are not necessary. Dogs intended for therapy work should know how to sit, down, heel, stay, and stand.

CHAPTER 20

The Senior Rottweiler

AT SOME POINT, YOU'RE GOING TO wake up one
morning and find that your rottie has gotten old. Oh,
you've noticed the little signs here or there: the gray on
the muzzle, the little bit of stiffness in the morning, the desire to
sleep in. But when did your rottie become old? Being old doesn't
mean being infirm. You can still do things with your rottweiler, but
now you just have to take it a little easier. In this chapter, we'll discuss the senior rottie and what you can expect. We'll also cover
the difficult decision of euthanasia.

How Old Is Old?

When does your rottweiler become old? That is a matter up for
debate because dogs age differently. This is the same with people.
Some look ancient when they're fifty, and some others look ter-
rific when they're in the seventies. Your rottie's longevity and the
quality of his life depend largely on genetics, diet, and exercise.
While genetics plays a role in a dog's life, whether you take advantage of good heredity is up to you. Your rottweiler can have the
most long-lived ancestors only to die at an early age, feeble and
inactive, because you kept him too fat and allowed him to become
a couch potato.

Don't be distressed at the thought of your rottie getting older.
Older dogs are often more enjoyable to have around. The puppy

destructiveness is gone, and you can often kick back and relax with your old friend.

Exercise

As with humans, exercise adds years to and even increases the quality of a dog's life. Exercise is important in the older dog. While your rottie may not feel like going on a long hike, you can certainly still take him for walks, play fetch, and even do some dog sports. Some agility trials have veteran's classes for the aging dog. However, as your rottweiler grows older, he is more susceptible to cancers, tumors, and other conditions. He may be more inclined to stretch out and snooze by the fire instead of waking you up for the early-morning walk. He may show stiffness due to arthritis.

Looking for Cancer

Always note the changes in your rottweiler's health. If you find any lumps or bumps that are not symmetrical—that is, your rottie does not have the same bump or lump on the other side in the same place—you should take him to the vet for an examination. A good time to examine your rottweiler is when you are grooming him. This way, you can learn what is normal and easily spot something abnormal, should it arise.

 **Fact**

Compared to humans, dogs have a short lifespan. Some rottweilers can live over ten years of age, but many start having problems when they're eight or nine. Much of your rottweiler's health depends on your care but also on his genetics.

Signs of Aging

Your rottweiler should start showing signs of aging somewhere between eight and ten years. This might include a little gray or white on the muzzle and perhaps a little cloudiness in the eyes. The eyes start changing at eight years of age. If you see cloudiness in the eyes, have your vet check them to be on the safe side. You don't want to mistake progressive retinal atrophy or glaucoma for normal aging.

Supplements

If your rottweiler is not active, you may see signs of arthritis early. Some supplements, such as glucosamine and MSM can help relieve arthritis. Do not give analgesics such as acetaminophen (Tylenol) or ibuprofen (Motrin, Advil); they are very poisonous to dogs. Your vet can prescribe the right amount of buffered aspirin, anti-inflammatories, or steroids to alleviate pain and swelling.

Diet

If your rottweiler is starting to gain weight, you may wish to cut back a little on his food. Unless he is inactive or has kidney disease, do not be tempted to switch him to a lower-protein or senior diet. Active dogs still require protein—even when they age. This is perhaps even more true if they are active, as their bodies must work harder to repair muscle and damaged tissue.

After Ten

After age ten, your rottie may still look healthy, or he may start aging rapidly. Observe any changes in diet, mood, or activity level and alert the vet. Incontinence is a sign of possible bladder or kidney problems and requires a trip to the vet. Spayed females may become incontinent as they grow older. If so, your vet has medications that can help.

Rottweiler life spans are usually between ten and thirteen years. Occasionally, you'll find a rottie that lives past thirteen, but that is rare. Enjoy your rottweiler's golden years together. If you keep him active and fit throughout his life, it should make them that much more enjoyable.

Keeping Your Old Rottie Comfortable

As your rottweiler gets older, he may find that sleeping in a crate or on the hard floor is uncomfortable. He would probably appreciate a soft, comfy dog bed. In the summer, a cool mat or a water-filled bed—yes, they make waterbeds for dogs!—might help keep him cool. Look for dog beds with orthopedic foam. They will help cushion your rottie's joints. However, if your rottweiler is still the aggressive chewer, you may find the bed shredded apart and water or foam all over the floor! So use common sense when looking to keep your old dog comfortable. If he is having trouble walking up and down the stairs because of arthritis, consider keeping him on the ground floor of the house. That way, you won't have to drag him up and down the stairs.

 Essential

There is equipment you can purchase to make your older dog's life easier. For instance, some manufacturers make ramps for older dogs so that they can walk into the car or climb up on the sofa without stressing their joints.

Age brings deafness as well as stubbornness. Go easy on the old guy, especially if he is acting particularly stubborn. You may have to shout your commands or use hand signals. Deteriorating eyesight is also a part of old age, so you may wish to hold off on redecorating the room or moving furniture around. Most blind dogs do exceptionally well—so well, in fact, that their owners may not know their dog is blind until the owner gets new furniture or moves to a new house.

Exercise is still very important to your rottweiler's health. Assuming there are no conditions or medical problems, continue to exercise him. However, you may find that he can no longer hike those ten miles with a twenty-pound pack. Lighten the load, and don't go as far. If you see him becoming tired, rest and turn back. You wouldn't take Grandpa on a twenty-mile forced march, so don't expect an old dog to do it, either.

You may end up being on a first-name basis with your vet as your rottweiler ages. At this stage, the key is comfort and quality of life. If, for example, your ten-year-old rottweiler develops osteosarcoma (bone cancer), you don't have many options. Opting for an aggressive treatment may or may not save your rottweiler's life, but it is also capable of causing a good deal of pain. The humane option would be to treat the disease as best you could, keeping in mind your rottweiler's comfort is the most important factor.

Arthritis

Arthritis is prevalent in older dogs. Luckily, there are various treatments available. The onset of arthritis depends largely on how active your dog is. Couch potatoes are more likely to develop arthritis earlier than dogs that are physically active throughout their lives.

Some supplements, such as glucosamine and MSM (found in Cosequin, Glycoflex, or Synova-Cre), can help relieve arthritis. These supplements work well on some dogs and do nothing for others. Your dog usually has to take these supplements for more than six weeks before you can see any effect.

 Fact

The later years may require a bit of change in your and your rottie's life. Your rottie's quality of life is very important. Be certain that your rottweiler isn't in pain and can still enjoy the things he used to.

Your vet can help mitigate some of the effects of arthritis with anti-inflammatories, such as nonsteroidal anti-inflammatory drugs (NSAIDS). Rimadyl, Metacam, Deramaxx, and Zubrin are some of the NSAIDS your veterinarian now has available. Aspirin is a common pain reliever; ask your vet for the proper dosage. The downside to NSAIDS is that some can adversely affect the kidneys and liver in some dogs. Dogs with sensitive stomachs can experience bleeding ulcers.

Steroids are another potential weapon against arthritis. These treatments can help bring relief and reduce inflammation, but they can have long-term drawbacks including immune-system suppression, increased appetite and weight, increased aggression, and increased water consumption and urination.

Cancer

Cancer and tumors are more prevalent with age. Cancer is the leading cause of death in dogs over eight years old. Although those numbers seem grim, 50 percent of all cancers and tumors are curable. Cancer is not an automatic death sentence.

If you find a lump or bump that isn't normally on your dog, have it checked immediately. Some cancers and tumors are fast spreading. If you wait too long, it may be too late for your veterinarian to do anything about them. Signs of cancer include strange growths, excessive weight loss, lack of appetite, bleeding, sores or wounds that will not heal, abnormal swellings, excessive sleep or lethargy, and difficulty breathing, eating, or drinking.

 **Alert!**

Before you opt for cancer treatment, ask your vet about the prognosis for full recovery. Is it going to completely cure your rottweiler, or will it buy him a few months? Some cancers are just not curable or very difficult to treat. It is a quality-of-life issue.

Veterinarians use a combination of techniques to battle cancer. Surgery, chemotherapy, and radiation have all been standard tools against cancer, but they have now been significantly improved and can be joined with other methods. Chemotherapy, long maligned for its side effects, now has some refinement. Using the latest DNA information, researchers have developed certain drugs that leave the healthy cells alone and aim specifically at the tumors and cancer. Cancer vaccines may offer hope that someday, once diagnosed with cancer, your dog may simply go in for a vaccination and have the body fight the cancer itself.

Loss of Senses

Your rottie may experience loss of senses, including eyesight, hearing, and even mental faculties. You may not even notice if your rottweiler goes blind. Most dogs are quite adept at getting around their home and even their neighborhood even though they're blind. The owner usually notices something is amiss when the dog bumps into something that normally isn't there. If you think your rottie has lost his sight, have your vet confirm your suspicions.

Blind dogs require a little more care than sighted dogs. Don't rearrange the furniture. Keep a blind dog at home and in familiar surroundings. Don't let him off the leash, or he might wander around and become lost. When in a strange place, keep him beside you so you can keep him safe.

Deafness

If your dog acts as if he's ignoring you, he may be going deaf. Deafness can come on gradually or suddenly. Clap your hands behind your dog's head, or rattle the food bowl while he's in the other room. If he doesn't react, he's probably deaf.

Deaf dogs can be exceedingly frustrating. You'll find yourself shouting at the dog for no good reason—as though your dog will hear you talking louder. The truth is that once the hearing goes, your rottie is unlikely to hear even shouting. Some deaf dogs can hear whistles, but some are just completely deaf.

If your rottie is deaf, you'll have to teach him hand signals. Start slowly. Teach him as you would a puppy. It may take a little bit of time for him to pick up on it, but most dogs are clever and can figure it out.

 **Esseñtial**

You may be surprised to learn that there are hearing aids available for dogs. These are still experimental and cutting-edge, but they are available if you think your dog might benefit from one. Ask your veterinarian.

Senility or Cognitive Dysfunction Syndrome

Cognitive dysfunction syndrome (CDS) is a canine version of Alzheimer's disease. CDS manifests itself with a marked change in behavior. Your dog may suddenly look lost in the room. He may not recognize loved ones and may forget his housetraining. His sleep may be disrupted, and he may bark and carry on in the middle of the night.

Brain tumors may mimic the symptoms of CDS, so it is very important to have a brain tumor ruled out first before CDS treatment. The CDS treatment of choice is Anipryl, which is also used to treat Cushing's disease in dogs. The therapy can be expensive, costing $50 to $100 a month, and only 60 percent of dogs show improvement. Once the dog is on the therapy, he must remain on it his entire life or symptoms will reappear.

Should You Get Another Dog?

Some people decide to get a puppy as their dog ages. The idea is to help mitigate the pain of losing the beloved pet when the time finally arrives. This can be good or bad, depending on the circumstance. If your rottweiler is very old, he may look on this new puppy as an interloper. A puppy will take most of your time and energy, leaving little time for your old dog. Your rottweiler may feel neglected and may become aggressive or short-tempered with your new pup.

 **Fact**

There are dogs that tolerate puppies well. Sometimes a puppy can spark new life into an old dog. Something new and exciting can shake an old dog from the routine enough to make him feel young again. Some older dogs are quick to become the puppy's aunt or uncle and are delighted to show the newcomer the ropes.

Whether another dog or puppy is accepted largely depends on you and your rottie. If your rottie gets along with other dogs and puppies, perhaps getting a puppy might be the right choice. At the same time, you must make the time to have your rottie feel extra special. Don't stop doing things with him now that you have the puppy; otherwise, he will associate the lack of attention with the appearance of the interloper.

▲ Would your adult rottweiler be pleased with a new friend?

When you introduce the two, always choose a neutral area such as a park. Let your rottweiler greet the newcomer while on leash. Praise him for good behavior, and discourage bad behavior. It may a take a few sessions before you can let your rottweiler loose with the other dog or puppy.

Saying Goodbye

The decision of when is the right time to say goodbye is a hard one. It is never easy to make the decision to euthanize a beloved pet. Your rottweiler may be old and feeble, unable to walk without your help, or might be lingering on from a terrible illness. Perhaps a car struck your rottweiler or he somehow became severely injured, and the prognosis looks grim. Whatever the reason, you may have to make the decision whether to euthanize your rottweiler.

Sometimes the decision to euthanize your pet is very clear-cut. Other times, the decision is not so clear. You may be sitting in an emergency room talking with the vet over possible courses of action. Heroic efforts may be required that cost far beyond what you can afford and that give your rottweiler only a very slim chance of recovery. In times like this, talk to someone you can trust—perhaps your own vet—or obtain a second opinion. Other friends who are dog owners may be able to see clearly when you cannot. They may offer you advice untainted by the emotions of the situation.

An End to Suffering

Whatever you decide, do not allow your best friend to suffer in pain needlessly. Your rottweiler deserves better than that. A painless injection will relieve his suffering. You can stay with your rottweiler during the euthanasia or leave. Many pet owners prefer to stay with their pet during their final moments. Your vet will give you the option of taking the body for burial or cremation. Check with zoning ordinances before burying your rottie in the backyard. Another option is burial in a pet cemetery. If you wish to have a cremation, you can request either to have the ashes returned to you for scattering or to place in an urn.

 **Essential**

Sometimes the decision to euthanize isn't clear-cut. Ask yourself if your rottie is able to eat, drink, move around, breathe, urinate, and defecate without pain. Is your rottie able to enjoy things, or is he just hanging on? Is he in pain that you can't mitigate? These are all important factors to consider when deciding to euthanize.

Grief

You will grieve. This is normal and natural. Do not talk to people who don't own pets, as they will be the most callous. "It was only a dog," they may say. "You can get another one." Or they may say the right things without sincerity. You don't need to hear this at this time. You will go through various stages of grief: anger, denial, depression, and then finally, acceptance. This is natural. Do not deny yourself a period of grieving. Your rottweiler was your friend and in many ways was probably more important to your life than a lot of people you know. It is normal to feel sadness over his death.

 **Fact**

Usually the most cost-efficient way of handling your rottie's remains is through a mass cremation. There is nothing wrong with this, and quite often the crematorium scatters the ashes on flowers growing nearby.

Talk to your vet about grief. He or she may be able to refer you to free or low-cost pet-loss counseling. Many veterinary colleges offer free or low-cost pet-loss hot lines. Another resource is the Internet. An excellent site for finding pet-loss support groups, hot lines, and information is *www.petloss.com*. Take care of yourself during this time. Keep busy and active. Exercise and eat a balanced diet. Avoid being alone and going into depression. You aren't denying that you have grief over the loss; you are helping yourself deal with it.

With time, the pain and anguish of your pet's death will fade. You will start remembering all the good times you had together. Perhaps, in time, you'll be ready to get another rottweiler. Perhaps you will get a puppy to keep you occupied. If you do, remember that no puppy will replace your beloved pet and that no other dog will be like your rottweiler. Your new puppy or dog will have a different personality and different behaviors, so do not expect the same thing out of this puppy. However, in time, you may grow to love this new addition as much as your beloved old pet.

Organizations

Agility Association of Canada (AAC)
RR #2
Lucan, Ontario, Canada
N0N2J0
(519) 657-7636

AKC Companion Animal Recovery
5580 Centerview Drive, Suite 250
Raleigh, NC 27606-3389
(800) 252-7894
Web site: *www.akccar.org*

American Kennel Club (AKC)
5580 Centerview Drive
Raleigh, NC 27606-3390
(919) 233-9767
Web site: *www.akc.org*
E-mail: *info@akc.org*

American Rottweiler Club Breed
Rescue
Attention: Gwen Chaney
5014 Granger Court
Indianapolis IN, 46268
(317) 280-1235
E-mail: *ejchaneyjr@aol.com*

American Rottweiler Club
(Carting)
Attention: Sandy Kinsman
830 Etchverry Street
Ramona, CA 93065
E-mail: *Rottentrackdogs@aol.com*

Australian Shepherd Club of
America (ASCA)
6091 East State Highway 21
Bryan, TX 77803-9652
(409) 778-1082
E-mail: *asca@mail.myraid.net*

Canine Eye Registration
Foundation (CERF)
Department of Veterinary Clinical
Science
School of Veterinary Medicine
Purdue University
West Lafayette, IN 47907
(765) 494-8179
Fax: (765) 494-9981
Web site:
www.vet.purdue.edu/~yshen/
cerf.html

Canine Freestyle Federation
Attention: Monica Patty,
Corresponding Secretary
21900 Foxden Lane
Leesburg, VA 20175
Web site: *www.canine-freestyle.org*
E-mail: *secretary@canine-freestyle.org*

Delta Society (Therapy Dogs)
289 Perimeter Road East
Renton, WA 98055-1329
(425) 226-7357
Web site: *www.deltasociety.org*
E-mail: *info@deltasociety.org*

DVG America (Schutzhund)
Attention: Sandi Purdy, Secretary
2101 South Westmoreland Road
Red Oak, TX 75154
(972) 617-2988
Web site: *www.dvgamerica.com*
E-mail: *Spurdy5718@aol.com*

**National Dog Groomers
Association of America**
P.O. Box 101
Clark, PA 16113
(724) 962-2711
E-mail: *ndga@nauticom.net*

National Dog Registry
Box 116
Woodstock, NY 12498
(800) 637-3647
Web site:
www.natldogregistry.com

**North American Dog Agility
Council (NADAC)**
HCR 2, Box 277
St. Maries, ID 83861
(208) 689-3803
Web site: *www.nadac.com*
E-mail: *nadack9@aol.com*

**North American Flyball
Association, Inc.**
1400 W. Devon Ave, #512
Chicago, IL 60660
(309) 688-9840
Web site: *www.flyball.org*
E-mail: *flyball@flyball.org*

**Orthopedic Foundation for Animals
(OFA)**
2300 Nifong Boulevard
Columbia, MO 65201
(573) 442-0418
Web site: *www.offa.org*

PennHIP
Synbiotics Corporation
11011 Via Frontera
San Diego, CA 92127
(858) 451-3771
Fax: (858) 451-5719
Web site:
*www.synbiotics.com/html/chd_penn
_hip.html*

Pet Assure
10 South Morris Street
Dover, NJ 07801
(888) 789-PETS
Web site: *www.petassure.com*
E-mail: *custserv@petassure.com*

PetCare Insurance Programs
P.O. Box 8575
Rolling Meadows, IL 60008
(866) 275-PETS
Web site:
www.petcareinsurance.com/us
E-mail: *info@petcareinsurance.com*

Pet Plan Insurance (Canada)
777 Portage Avenue
Winnipeg, MB, R3G 0N3 Canada
(905) 279-7190
Web site: *www.petplan.com*

Petshealth Insurance Agency
P.O. Box 2847
Canton, OH 44720
(888) 592-7387
Web site:
www.petshealthplan.com

Premier Pet Insurance Group
9541 Harding Boulevard
Wauwatosa, WI 53226
(877) 774-2273
Web site: *www.ppins.com*

Tattoo-A-Pet
6571 SW 20th Court
Ft. Lauderdale, FL 33317
(800) 828-8667
Web site: *www.tattoo-a-pet.com*

Therapy Dogs International, Inc.
Attention: New Registrations
88 Bartley Road
Flanders, NJ 07836
(973) 252-9800
Web site: *www.tdi-dog.org*
E-mail: *tdi@gti.net*

United Kennel Club (UKC)
100 East Kilgore Road
Kalamazoo, MI 49001-5593
Web site: *www.ukcdogs.com*

The United Schutzhund Clubs of America
3810 Paule Avenue
St. Louis, MO 63125-1718
(314) 638-9686
Fax: (314) 638-0609
Web site:
www.germanshepherddog.com

United States Dog Agility Association (USDAA)
P.O. Box 850955
Richardson, TX 75085-0955
(972) 231-9700
Information Line: (888) AGILITY
Web site: *www.usdaa.com*
E-mail: *info@usdaa.com*

Veterinary Pet Insurance (VPI)
P.O. Box 2344
Brea, CA 92822
(800) USA-PETS
Web site: *www.petinsurance.com*

World Canine Freestyle Organization Ltd.
P.O. Box 250122
Brooklyn, NY 11235
(718) 332-8336
Fax: (718) 646-2686
Web site: *www.woofs.org*
E-mail: *wcfodogs@aol.com*

APPENDIX B

Periodicals and Books

Periodicals

AKC Gazette
51 Madison Avenue
New York, NY 10010

Dog Fancy Magazine
P.O. Box 53264
Boulder, CO 80322-3264
(800) 365-4421
Web site: *www.dogfancy.com*

Dog World
P.O. Box 56240
Boulder, CO 80323-6240
(800) 361-8056

Books

Adelman, Beth and Fodors, eds. *Mobil 2004 Travel Guide on the Road with Your Pet: More Than 4,400 Mobil-Rated Lodgings in North America for Travelers with Dogs, Cats, and Other Pets.* (Mobil Travel Guide: On the Road with Your Pet, Mobil Oil Corporation, 2004).

Alderton, David. *The Dog Care Manual.* (Hauppauge, NY: Barron's Educational Series, 1986).

American Automotive Association. *Traveling with Your Pet—The AAA PetBook*, 5th edition. (AAA, 2003).

American Kennel Club. *The Complete Dog Book,* 19th edition revised. (New York: Howell Book House, 1997).

Arden, Andrea, and Emmanuelle Morgan, ed. *Fodor's Road Guide USA: Where to Stay with Your Pet (Fodor's Road Guide USA: Where to Stay with Your Pet).* (Fodor, 2001).

Benjamin, Carol Lea. *Second-Hand Dog.* (New York: Howell Book House, 1988).

Bonham, Margaret H. *An Introduction to Dog Agility.* (Hauppauge, NY: Barron's Educational Series, 2000).

Bonham, Margaret H. *The Simple Guide to Getting Active with Your Dog.* (Neptune City, NJ: TFH Publications Inc, 2002).

Bonham, Margaret H., and James M. Wingert, D.V.M. *The Complete Idiot's Guide to Dog Health and Nutrition.* (Indianapolis, IN: Alpha Books, 2003).

Coffman, Howard D. *The Dry Dog Food Reference.* (Nashua, NH: Pig Dog Press, 1995).

Eldredge, Debra, D.V.M. *Pills for Pets.* (New York: Citadel Press, 2003).

Fogle, Bruce, D.V.M. *The New Encyclopedia of the Dog.* (New York: DK Books, 2000).

Giffin, James M., M.D., and Liisa D. Carlson, D.V.M. *The Dog Owner's Home Veterinary Handbook,* 3rd edition. (New York: Howell Book House, 2000).

Grayson, Fred N., and Chris Kingsley. *The Portable petswelcome.com: The Complete Guide to Traveling with Your Pet.* (New York: Howell Book House, 2001).

Habgood, Dawn, and Robert Habgood. *Pets on the Go: The Definitive Pet Accommodation and Vacation Guide.* (Duxbury, MA: Dawbert Press, 2002).

James, Ruth B., D.V.M., *The Dog Repair Book.* (Mills, WY: Alpine Press, 1990).

Klever, Ulrich. *The Complete Book of Dog Care.* (Hauppauge, NY: Barron's Educational Series, 1989).

LaBelle, Charlene. *A Guide to Backpacking with Your Dog.* (Loveland, CO: Alpine Publications, 1993).

Martin Management Books. *Great Vacations for You & Your Dog, USA, 2003–04.* (Martin Management Books, 2003).

Streitferdt, Uwe. *Healthy Dog, Happy Dog.* (Hauppauge, NY: Barron's Educational Series, 1994).

Volhard, Joachim, Wendy Volhard, and Jack Volhard. *The Canine Good Citizen: Every Dog Can Be One.* (New York: Howell Book House, 1997).

Zink, M. Chris, D.V.M., Ph.D. *Peak Performance, Coaching the Canine Athlete.* (New York: Howell Book House).

Index

We have ...

EVERYTHING

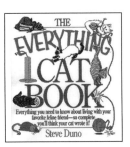
Have you ever wondered how to tempt your finicky cat to eat, or how to put that fat cat on a diet? What is the best way to keep your cat from eating your house plants? You'll find the answers to these and many other questions in *The Everything® Cat Book*. From choosing a veterinarian and basic first-aid to fascinating cat lore and trivia, this title offers everything you need to know about living with your favorite feline friend.

Whether you're the proud owner of a registered pure-bred Jack Russell Terrier or a happy-go-lucky mutt from the pound, it's the one book you'll turn to again and again. Packed with illustrations, instructions, historical information, and useful tips, *The Everything® Dog Book* covers everything from training to breed behavior, from grooming to exercise, from traveling with your pooch to keeping him from destroying your slippers.

As every dog owner knows, it takes a lot of time and patience to train a dog—and even more to get him to do tricks and show off in front of friends. In *The Everything® Dog Training and Tricks Book*, Canine University® cofounder Gerilyn Bielakiewicz explains how to solve virtually every behavioral issue—from aggressiveness to digging—and guides you through teaching all kinds of feats, whether your dog is in "kindergarten" or has graduated to "circus dog."

...for Pets!

This exciting book is perfect for horse lovers of all ages and skill levels. You'll learn what breed is best suited to a rider's needs and skills, as well as how to buy a horse, how to choose a reliable vet, and how to detect early symptoms of various health issues. Packed with professional suggestions, horse trivia, and definitions of equine jargon, *The Everything® Horse Book* would make an ideal gift for anyone who has ever been interested in our equestrian friends.

Trade paperback,
$14.95 ($22.95 CAN)
1-58062-564-9, 304 pages

Trade paperback,
$14.95 ($22.95 CAN)
1-58062-576-2, 320 pages

Nothing is more adorable than a new puppy! But no matter how cute, puppies take a lot of hard work and loving care. *The Everything® Puppy Book* teaches you absolutely everything you need to raise your precious pet through the most critical stages of his or her life. Including photographs of your favorite breeds and a color insert, this book covers everything from grooming to exercise, and training to breed behavior.

Whether you are interested in fresh water or salt water tropical fish, *The Everything® Tropical Fish Book* is a complete resource for creating environments for fish to thrive. In this book, readers will find complete descriptions of various species, from freshwater goldfish and koi to rare tropical breeds. There are hundreds of tips on how to choose the right fish for every aquarium, and subsequently feed, breed, and maintain them.

Trade paperback,
$14.95 ($22.95 CAN)
1-58062-343-3, 320 pages
plus 8-page color insert

Other

EVERYTHING
DOG BREED GUIDES

THE

EVERYTHING
GOLDEN RETRIEVER

B O O K

A complete guide to raising, training, and caring for your Golden

Gerilyn J. Bielakiewicz & Paul S. Bielakiewicz
cofounders of Canine University®

Trade Paperback
ISBN: 1-59337-047-4
$12.95 ($19.95 CAN)

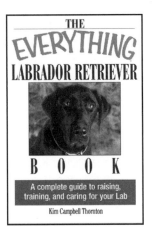

THE

EVERYTHING
LABRADOR RETRIEVER

B O O K

A complete guide to raising, training, and caring for your Lab

Kim Campbell Thornton

Trade Paperback
ISBN: 1-59337-048-2
$12.95 ($19.95 CAN)

THE

EVERYTHING
POODLE

B O O K

A complete guide to raising, training, and caring for your Poodle

Janine Adams

Trade Paperback
ISBN: 1-59337-121-7
$12.95 ($19.95 CAN)

Available wherever books are sold!
To order, call 800-872-5627,
or visit us at *www.everything.com*

Everything® and everything.com® are registered trademarks of F+W Publications, Inc.